The Ten Divine Articles of Sri Durga

Insights and Meditations

D0869960

Babaji Bob Kindler

SARADA RAMAKRISHNA VIVEKANANDA ASSOCIATIONS OF
OREGON, SAN FRANCISCO, & HAWAII

Other works by Babaji Bob Kindler
We Are Atman All-Abiding
Strike Off Thy Fetters
Hasta-Amalaka Stotram
Twenty-Four Aspects of Mother Kali
The Avadhut And His Twenty-Four Teachers In Nature
Sri Sarada Vijnanagita

Copyright 1996, 2001 by Babaji Bob Kindler.
First Edition 1996. Second printing 1996.
Third printing 2001, new edition.
ISBN 1-891893-07-6
All rights reserved.
Published by SRV Associations of Oregon, San Francisco, & Hawaii

For further information write to:
SRV Oregon
P.O. Box 14012
Portland, OR 97293 USA
(503) 774-2410
srvinfo@srv.org
or
SRV Retreat Center
PO Box 380
Paauilo, HI 96776 USA
srvhawaiirc@srv.org

Cover Art: Sri Durga Mahishasura

Production by Lokelani Kindler
Illustrations and proofing by Annapurna Sarada
Digital Imaging by Prem Durga Marisela Bracho

The publication of this book was made possible by donations from friends and students of the independent SRV Associations.

Sri Durga Devi

Sri Durga Gayatri Om, Katyayanaya Vidmahe
Kanya Kumari Dhimahi, Tan No Durgah Prachodayat
Om Durga Devi Namaha

Contents

Preface

The fascinating and compelling image of Sri Durga, the Divine Mother of the Universe in Her ten-armed aspect who epitomizes Absolute Power, is the subject of this presentation. I realize that I have chosen a subject that defies description and which transcends all attempts to comprehend with the mind, but it is precisely for this reason that I am embarking on this task. Knowing that it is impossible to cover all bases leaves one free of trying to include every little fact and bit of knowledge into a work about the transcendent Universal Mother who is, after all, extremely subtle by nature and infinite by design. Additionally, this literary journey allows me to offer spontaneous insights that have emerged from 25 years of formal meditation upon the Universal Mother, permeated by my heart's love for Her, my Chosen Ideal.

There are so many things which this powerful aspect of Universal Motherhood encompasses. I mentioned above the awesome principle of Absolute Power in particular due to the many references to this quality in sacred scripture, but Sri Durga incorporates all qualities within Her incomprehensible scope because She is first and foremost among Divine Beings. In the *Srimad Devi Bhagavatam*, the Divine Mother principle is christened with the epithet of *Mula Prakriti*, which transmits such meanings as the primeval root, the subtle foundation, the underlying substratum, the primal awareness, and the very essence of existence. It is given that the word *Prakriti*, usually understood by limited thinkers to refer to physical nature alone, has three subtle meanings.

First, dividing it into two parts, its prefix, *"Pra,"* denotes what is superior and extremely exalted while its affix, *"Kriti,"* implies creation — that which is secondary or subordinate to the ultimate principle. Dividing the word into its three syllables, *"Pra"* represents the *sattva guna* (equipoise), *"Kri"* signifies *rajo guna* (frenetic activity) and *"Ti"* symbolizes the *tamo guna* (inertia). Finally, to emphasize that the Universal Mother is never limited to the modes of creation, preservation and destruction, it is pointed out that the syllable *"Pra"* means that which is anterior to all manifestation and the syllable *"Kri"* stands for the appearance of the universe itself. As the *Srimad Devi Bhagavatam* explains:

"When this Intelligence of the nature of Brahma, beyond the three attributes (gunas), gets tinged with the above three gunas and becomes omnipotent, then She is superior in the work of creation. Hence She is styled Prakriti. O child Narada! The state just preceding that of creation is denoted by 'Pra' and 'Kri' signifies creation. So the great Devi who exists before creation is called Prakriti after creation."

From this inconceivable title — *Mula Prakriti* — springs the five main manifestations of Her ever-unified being called *Prakriti Panchaka*. These inseparable divine expressions comprise the sanctified circle of Goddesses who oversee every aspect of the creation.

There is Padma, Sri Lakshmi, the Mother granting all wealth and abundance, both terrestrial and spiritual, who is reverently referred to as *Sattva Shuddha* due to the fact that She transcends the highest principles. Then there is Saraswati — all white, all pure — who embodies and confers all knowledge, both sacred and secular. Savitri is worshipped as well, for She is the Mother of austerities, the root of all mantras and their meanings which bring association and communion with various divine personages and principles. Importantly, there is Sri Radha, the Mother of *prana*, the essence of life and love and the presiding deity of the Supreme Lord, Sri Krishna.

Each one of these predominant aspects of the Goddess occupies a unique position and deserves special attention, but Sri Durga is mentioned first. The reason for this is brought out in the *Srimad Devi Bhagavatam:*

"Durga, the Mother of Ganesh, comes, as the first, the most auspicious, loved by Shiva. She is Narayani, Vishnu Maya, and the nature of Purna Brahma (the Supreme Brahma). This eternal and all-pervading Devi is the presiding deity of all the devas and is therefore worshipped and praised by all devas, munis and manus. This Bhagavati Durga Devi, when She gets pleased, destroys all sorrows, pains and troubles of the bhaktas that have taken Her refuge and gives them karma, everlasting name and fame, all auspicious things, bliss and all happiness — nay, the final liberation!"

Thus we begin to apprehend the importance of knowing as much as possible about the Supreme Mother of the Universe appearing as Sri Durga Devi. Far too little is known about Her and what little of this is available comes promise and blind faith.

This type of philosophy is unacceptable, is a form of separation from Her, is a way of purposefully or unconsciously distancing ourselves from the Truth that She so clearly embodies. After all, She is the Wisdom Mother, and Wisdom emanates from Truth and manifests in our world and to our minds as knowledge. Taking recourse to this knowledge in ascending fashion, human beings remove ignorance from the mind and gradually rise above all limitations. As the holy scriptures declare, *"She exists as medha — Intelligence."* How else are we to understand Her, if not by engendering intelligence within ourselves? Ramprasad, puts it in another way:

"Struggle to fathom Her, O mind, with every fiber of your energy. Your intelligence will be purified, but you will never understand Her." [2]

All attempts to know the Universal Mother would logically begin with a reverent examination of Her blessed form, so replete with profuse symbology and literally crying out for explanation. As has been mentioned, only cryptic references about the Divine Mother's presence and purpose are available, and these are buried deep and scattered throughout the few hoary and voluminous scriptural texts which exist on Mother worship. Therefore, the whys and wherefores concerning Her mission and meaning are mysteriously and unjustifiably missing. Perhaps this is due to the fact that Her worship and acknowledgment has for so long been denied or overlooked and that She is only recently re-emerging from the depths of the collective heart and memory of humanity, assuming again Her obvious and regal position as the

Mother of all souls.

Whatever the case may be, She has now arrived and is present among us and Her illumined and ecstatic children are rejoicing at this advent. This is instanced by the initial wealth of inspiring information, both practical and mystical, that has surfaced recently. My dear friend, Lex Hixon, who on November 1st (Jagaddhatri Puja and All Saints day) merged his entire being in the Divine Mother's boundless Consciousness, has written several unique books about Her such as *Mother of the Universe, Mother of the Buddhas,* and *Great Swan — Meetings with Ramakrishna.* Other works from other authors and devotees are also emerging as this enigmatic figure makes Herself known in various ways to the world in general.

The Ten Divine Articles of Sri Durga, as well as the *Twenty-Four Aspects of Mother Kali,* provide an introduction to the ultimate Goddess, both on a formal and a personal level. *The Ten Divine Articles* involve an in-depth exploration of the symbolism associated with the many objects seen in Sri Durga's lovely hands, and proceeds to utilize these many attributes as spiritual and devotional aids in a set of guided meditations. This study and its process is based upon the important premise that the divine articles held aloft in Her ten hands are not just physical objects, not only weapons for fighting negativity and not merely powers for bringing about benefit to struggling and aspiring beings. Each one is an inseparable and intrinsic portion of Her very nature, being extensions of Her infinite attributes and qualities in outer manifestation only. If this is comprehended and accepted at the outset, the reading and study of this work — even a mere perusal of its pages — will prove to be much more effective in conveying its essential inner message.

This perennial message is spiritual in nature, transforming in effect and inherently one with the Universal Mother. As the written word, its letters, its sound and the meaning connected with it are all one and inseparable, so too is the Universal Mother's transmission of Truth everunified and homogenous. In this way also are the ten articles that She carries indivisible parts of Her. The Sword, the Conch, the Discus, the Mala, the Bell, the Winecup, the Shield, the Bow, the Arrow and the Spear — they are all sublime expressions and nondual essences simultaneously. Being associated with Her, they act as purifying and enlightening forces coming straight from the Mother of the Universe. It is up to each of us, then, to gaze upon them, contemplate them, extract the meaning which they represent, implement this valuable information into our understanding and meditate in unified fashion upon the Beloved One who wields them endearingly with infinite care and perfect detachment.

Babaji Bob Kindler

Insights

The Ten Divine Articles of Sri Durga

Sri Durga is probably the most widely accepted aspect of *Shakti,* the creative energy of *Brahman,* Absolute Reality. From the standpoint of scriptural history, called Itihasa, She acquired Her powerful name by slaying the evil, ancient and ferocious demon named Durgama. Her name has also been translated as "She who is difficult to know." This is understandable since She is the Mother of all gods and goddesses, embodying the essential and most refined levels of Consciousness that are most difficult of access. Her precise and timely appearances during times of crisis also indicate Her subtlety, for even the highest gods are seldom privileged enough to be graced by Her visitation. The *Srimad Devi Bhagavatam,* one of the few quintessential Divine Mother scriptures, tries often to explain the apparent dichotomy of Her evasive yet ever-present nature:

"O Mother! Thou art the merciful Mother of the three worlds; Thou art the adorable auspicious Vidya (knowledge) benefiting all the Lokas; Thou destroyest the Universe and Thou skillfully residest (hidden) in the Vija mantras. Therefore we are praising Thee. O Mother! Brahma, Vishnu, Maheshvara, Indra, Surya, Agni, Sarasvati and the other regents of the Universe are all Thy creations; so none of them is superior to Thee. Thou art the Mother of all things, movable and unmovable.

"O Mother! When Thou dost will to create this visible Universe, Thou createst first Brahma, Vishnu, and Maheshvara and makest them create, preserve, and destroy this universe, but Thou remainest quite unattached to this world. Ever Thou remainest constant in Thy one form. No one in this Universe is able to know Thy nature, nor is there anybody who can enumerate Thy names. O Bhagavati! No one amongst the Devas even knows particularly Thy endless power and glory. Thou alone are the Lady of the Universe and the Mother of the Worlds.

"The Vedas all bear testimony how Thou alone hast created all this unreal and fleeting Universe. O Devi! Thou, without any effort and having no desires hast become the cause of this visible world, Thyself remaining unchanged. This is a great wonder. We cannot conceive of this combination of contrasting varieties in one. O Mother! How can we understand Thy power, unknown to all the Vedas even, when Thou Thyself hast not known the extent of Thy own nature! We are bewildered at this...." [3]

Mother Durga's essential nature, then, is unfathomable. However, when She intends to manifest Her beneficial powers for the good of Her creation, She fashions celestial and human mechanisms and enters into them as consciousness. Numerous are Her appearances throughout history, many lost in the distant recesses of time. One famous and ancient story tells of Her descent into form to rescue the gods and goddesses from evil and destruction. In this rendering, She chose to manifest a portion of Her infinite power through Brahma, Vishnu, Shiva and the entire divine pantheon. Each of these powerful beings combined their highest force of thought through a concentrated beam of conscious Light to aid in Her appearance. Each also offered Her an exact replica of his own personal preferred weapon of battle. In this fashion was the perfect Warrior Goddess born again, ready to dispel evil and all its legions.

Goddess Durga utilizes Her perfect prowess as a warrioress for the good of Her precious spiritual children. Every speck of consciousness in the Universe is under Her constant supervision, for Her essence is pure Consciousness and Consciousness is everywhere, being all-pervasive. As the ten-armed Goddess, She presents a radiantly beautiful form that is bewitching to behold. That special form is somehow simultaneously wrathful and benign and transmits profound spiritual teachings in an exacting manner with meticulous skill. The growth which proceeds from these teachings, beneficial or excruciating as the case may be, always results in the highest good. Her entire spectrum of activities gets accomplished with a boundless compassion and unconditional love that is too far-reaching for mortals to comprehend. Her august presence, full of incredible sweetness and intense power, is so auspicious as to warrant description of an entire *Purana*. A well-known and voluminous epic of over seven hundred mantras entitled the *Devi Mahatmyam* or *Durgasaptasati,* better known as the *Chandi,* has also been dedicated at Her feet of perfection. In these great works, Sri Durga is praised for Her extensive attributes and qualities through holy names which are attracting indeed to Her loving devotees but which are fear-inspiring to all the negative forces dwelling in the Universe.

As pure Consciousness Sri Durga exists eternally,

always abiding in Her own sweet nature. She also inhabits the hearts and minds of Her ecstatic devotees. As *shakti* power, She shapes, nurtures, and dissolves names and forms, while as subtle spiritual energy called *Kundalini*, She lights the lotuses of the seven centers of awareness in the sacred human body. It is only by supplicating Her that human beings can escape the snares of *Maya* (illusion, ignorance) and attain the rare boon of *Brahmajnana* (knowledge of God). The scriptures outline Her as being the essence and embodiment of divine qualities which are reflected in Her children, such as *smriti* (memory), *buddhi* (intelligence), *daya* (compassion), *samadhi* (ecstasy), and *prema* (pure love), to name a few. The boundless power that shapes and destroys entire solar systems is duly contained within Her and by Her indomitable will all things come into existence, are sustained, and disappear, dissolving back into Her infinite being.

Before describing the power, purpose, and symbology of Her Sword of Wisdom, a brief description of Her auspicious appearance should be given. She is usually pictured as having ten arms holding Sword, Conch, Discus, Rosary, Bell, Winecup, Shield, Bow, Arrow, and Spear. She is most often shown riding a lion from which comes Her august name, *Simhavahini,* "She who stands astride the king of beasts." She is gorgeously dressed in royal red cloth and has several ornaments decorating Her personage. Her hair is dressed up in a crown *(karandamukuta)* which then flows out in long luxuriant tresses that are darkly luminous and soothing to the eye. The ornaments adorning Her consist of armbands on each arm, a crown of gold and jewels encircling Her hair, earrings, a belt of bells about Her waist, and rings of bells around Her ankles.   Many gold wristbands encircle every arm except for the arms holding Spear and Shield which are protected by two forearm shields.   Her arms, neck, midsection, and feet are bare and Her dark amber skin is radiant and alluringly fragrant.   Her hair has no restricting ornaments but flows out long and free behind Her while retaining perfect order.   A golden aura, like the combined glow of many suns, engulfs Her visage and Her countenance is both peaceful and awe-inspiring.

The Sword of Nondual Wisdom

Sri Durga's legendary Sword of Nondual Wisdom is a weapon with three primary functions. It protects consciousness, destroys ignorance and promotes growth. Primarily, though, it represents the supremacy of nondual wisdom or Absolute Truth, for when ignorance disappears from the mind, its innate purity as limitless Awareness shines through naturally. The Mother's sword represents that most thorough power of scrutiny called mature discrimination that destroys ignorance and illusion immediately, leaving intelligence free to contemplate its own pristine nature. Even pervasive delusions born of the most tenacious negativity are ultimately dispelled by a stroke from the Divine Mother's Sword of Wisdom. This is why the Mother's sword is double-edged, for it is both destroyer and healer. It sweeps downward in its descending arc, cutting away the numerous layers of restricting limitations that cloud the intellect. Illusory superimpositions,[4] erroneous ideas and misconceptions, obsolete concepts and theories, confusing doubts, antiquated codes of conduct, binding attachments, detrimental desires, and other obstructions are all cut away at the root, leaving the field of awareness free of impediments.

As the Wisdom Mother raises Her precious weapon to its original, elevated position once again, its ascending

arc flashes in the sunlight of knowledge, conferring star-
tling insights proceeding from the boons of discrimination
and detachment. In this way, Her sword not only destroys
but creates anew and restores a natural and peaceful
atmosphere to the troubled mind. This powerful process
that facilitates the destruction of ignorance and egoism
(ahamkara), further entails the purification of the mind's
subtle levels, the enlightenment of the intellect (buddhi),
and the refinement of the mind's consciousness (chitta).
This represents a substantial transformation and only
those sincere and devoted aspirants who strongly desire
perfection will offer their minds to the Universal Mother
for such major alterations. For those who succeed in con-
summating this ultimate offering, the Wisdom Eye gracing the sword's surface opens with astonishing clarity.
Illumined beings who are thus consecrated to their ideal
of the Universal Mother see, as it were, through this all-
seeing eye, being present for and fully aware of the amazing insights which materialize when the Sword of
Nondual Wisdom cleaves through the coverings of ignorance which veil Reality. These fortunate beings live on
the cutting edge of spontaneous insight and immediate
perception through the Mother's boundless Grace.
Offering their head and mind is therefore a wise decision,
for this type of subtle and symbolic decapitation results
in the attainment of the highest state of Awareness.

   This, then, is the explanation and symbology behind
the often perplexing spectacle of the severed head and
bloody sword which Mother Kali holds in Her two left
hands.   Only a total offering of all thoughts to the
Universal Mother will put an end to doubts and accomplish a blissful transcendence of the problems inherent in

relativity. Therefore, Her devotees offer Her their heads, complete with all thoughts, desires, dreams and intentions. The peaceful expression spread across the face of the severed head held in Mother's capable hand indicates that all nagging considerations that are characteristic of a mind steeped in ignorance have been put to rest. It is little wonder that the loving devotees of the Divine Mother of the Universe look upon Her Sword of Wisdom as an instrument that confers peace, bliss, truth, and freedom, and stand ready for its descending arc with expectant anticipation.

There are other striking features about the Wisdom Sword that warrant attention. Its constitution alone is exceptional and it possesses an aura all its own. Forged in the transcendental furnace of *Brahman*, formed from the steel of discrimination and detachment, subjected to the fire of supreme intelligence and cooled in the pure waters of perfect compassion, its very existence reveals the forces of *Maya* to be illusory. Its presence therefore insures the liberation of all beings from the impositions of duality and the *"illusion of finitude."* Since its swift stroke causes the demise of ignorance and the birth of knowledge, even the most pervasive delusions such as those involving fear and death are destroyed by its keen cutting edge. Thus, it is viewed as a weapon of nonduality, an instrument of unity, a path to freedom. Fallacious ideas associated with perpetual change and fluctuation, tendencies towards selfish clinging to finite forms, preoccupation with superficiality and mundane existence, and obsession with crippling desires and material possessions — these and other things born of a thirst for individual, sense-oriented experience cannot bear the radiant presence of the Universal Mother's ever-victorious weapon. Purification, transformation and transcendence are the irrepressible results of its timely application. The master-craftsman who formed this tool for enlightenment was an illumined knower of Brahman and an eternal devotee of the Divine Mother. This is indicated by the presence of certain powerful Sanskrit runes inlaid into its shining surface. The Divine Mother's own *bija mantras* are emblazoned there, permeating and empowering the sword with Her own dynamic power and essence. These quintessential seed syllables, *Om, Aim, Hrim,* impregnated with subtle spiritual intensity, are intrinsically and perpetually associated with the many divine names of the Goddess and act as invocations that usher the Universal Mother's presence into the hearts and minds of sincere beings. In *The Nine Limbs of Devotion According to Sri Ramchandra,* these auspicious and ancient symbols are discussed in relation to Mother Durga's Sword:

"The primordial nondual sword of Kali/Durga has the powerful combination Om, Aim, Hrim etched into its surface, denoting that purifying wisdom, transformation and transcendence are Her most precious boons. These also indicate Her adamant resolve and ultimate intent. She lofts this heavy and powerfully effective double-edged weapon over Her head as She strides onto the battleground of multiplicity and applies it to the task of obliterating the demonic forces that support the illusion of relativity and oppose unity. Pervasive delusion, egocentricity and individuality, all forms of pride and vanity, bestiality, the six passions[5] and their resultant effects — all will be annihi-

lated with exacting skill and characteristic detachment." [6]

The *Srimad Devi Bhagavatam* refers often to the power of the bija mantras, particularly that of Mother's precious *Hrim.* Its efficacy in removing ignorance and bestowing discernment leading to nondual wisdom is unsurpassed. By understanding the force of this bija with its symbol etched into the brilliant surface of this sacred weapon, an idea of its power can be comprehended. The Devi Herself speaks of this bija's power to transmit illumination, thereby accenting its importance:

"This Reality that I have spoken of is most excellent and is my Extraordinary Form. In the Vedas it is known as unmodified and unmanifested (Avyakrita and Avyakta), the Maya Shabala divided into many parts. In all the Shastras it is stated to be the Cause of all causes, the Primeval Tattva and the Satchitananda Vigraha. Where all the karmas are solidified and where Iccha Shakti (will), Jnana Shakti (intelligence), and Kriya Shakti (action) all are melted into one, that is called the Mantra Hrim. That is the first Tattva (principle). From out of this comes Akasha, having the property of sound, thence air with touch, fire with form, water with taste, and lastly earth having the quality of smell." [7]

Elsewhere in the *Srimad Devi Bhagavatam*, Hrim is called the *Hrillekha* mantram and confers the utmost sanctity. The Devi Herself states:

"The Hrillekha Mantra is the chief of all mantrams, so My worship and all other actions ought to be performed with this Hrillekha Mantram. I am always reflected in this mirror of Hrillekha form, so anything offered in this

Hrillekha Mantra of Mine is offered as it were with all the mantras."

The powerful symbology of the Divine Mother's sword reveals it as an efficacious tool that represents the destruction of ignorance on all levels of consciousness. Nor does its influence end here. An even fuller appreciation for it dawns when it is perceived as an instrument that facilitates the appearance and expression of many interrelated schools of knowledge, making accessible the infinite sets of methods that they offer to seekers of Truth. Some of these will be discussed at length throughout the pages of this book. The sword, more than any other article that the Mother carries, assumes paramount importance, for it seeks out obstacles to spiritual growth, discovers them concealed within the human heart and mind, selects the proper methods for doing away with them and destroys them in due course. It therefore flashes brilliantly on the field of battle, illuminates the corners of the mind where ignorance hides, guides the preceptor to that locale, advises the perfect course of action and deals the fatal stroke of death to the doubts, imperfections and limitations which inhabit human consciousness. The Wisdom Sword, then, epitomizes the path, the obstructions along the path, the method by which impediments along the path are removed, the teacher who removes the obstructions which allow for growth and progress along the path, and finally, the attainment of enlightenment — the arrival at the ultimate destination which is the true goal of human existence.

For embodied beings abiding within the confines of relative existence, dwelling in the spheres of name and form, Mother's Wisdom Sword represents spiritual life itself. To complete the integral description of Mother Durga's powerful appearance however, nine other divine articles must be discussed. These are the Conch, the Discus, the Mala (rosary), the Bell, the Winecup, the Shield, the Spear, the Bow, and the Arrow.

The Conch Shell of Auspicious Victory

The Conch Shell is a particularly amazing representation, pregnant with sacred symbology. Primarily, it suggests the auspiciousness of all creation. On more subtle levels, it equates to *bindu, nada, kalatita* — the initial seed, the primordial sound, and the web of time. At the surface of consciousness, where the pairs of opposites are constantly at war, it signifies the power of unification which causes all diversity to coalesce and merge in harmony. These three functions or meanings are all combined within Divine Mother's sacred Conch Shell.

The awesome beauty of the universal play, the thrill of dynamic action, and the experience of exaltation which proceeds from absolute victory — these are elements called forth by the thought of Mother Durga's Conch. In ancient times, the sound of the conch emanated forth on special occasions, both solemn and celebrative, while the sounding of multiple conch shells were used in battle to both inspire the warriors and to instill fear into the hearts and minds of the enemy. They were also sounded at the end of battle to signal an end to conflagration and to usher in periods of peaceful repose. The call to action, the intensity of interaction, and the merging of all activity into contrasting episodes of silence are all aptly expressed and strung together in sequence by the thread of tone emanating from the sacred conch shell. Therefore is it seen as a unifying principle symbolizing harmony. All things experienced or expressed during cyclic periods of creative activity are also suggested by the conch shell's existence and its pervasive vibration. That one long inspiring perfect tone, when heard deeply from within, suggests the beauty of nature, the play of the senses, and the infinite attributes of consciousness sporting throughout the universe. The scriptures of the Goddess indicate that the five elements — water, fire, earth, air, and ether — and their part in the creation of the worlds, are signified by the conch shell. Formed of the fires of creation from the materials of earth, immersed in ocean waters, filled with air, and possessed of a shape conducive to manifest sound through the ethers, the Universal Mother's perfect design epitomizes elemental essence. The hands which grasp it, the eyes which admire its shape and surface, the nose and mouth which draw and expel breath through it, and the ears which thrill to its elevating sound, are all testaments to the existence of the senses and their integral part in the experience of life.

There are also deep subtle and metaphysical meanings associated with this divine article. The conch shell's subtle nature is represented by its association with vibration, while its mystical condition is revealed through its association with creation, preservation and dissolution. These two aspects are closely related. Placing an ear over the shell's opening, one can hear a sound within, though there is no apparent cause. This is a microcosm example of the existence of a subtle unseen reality existing within all things. In this way, the sacred conch delivers up a precious secret — that the universe is born of vibration. By the sweet will of *Ishvara*, the Supreme Being as Creator, Preserver and Destroyer of the Universe, the first vibration is sent forth across the expanse of formless consciousness. Other vibrations spring from the original and the once calm ocean of potential manifestation suddenly sports a surface full of activity-waves, all interacting with one another. The ocean is now a riot of surface turmoil as manifestation plays and sports in a seemingly unending succession of cyclic interactions. Finally, after the waves have played out their dance, after the energy of cause and effect has been exhausted, peace returns and reigns supreme. Through all of this, the depths of this ocean have remained unchanged, calm and serene, unaffected by the conflagration occurring on its surface.

Within the conch shell, then, is the subtle sound, uncaused by any obvious presence, yet suggesting the existence of an unseen power possessing the potential to unleash, manipulate, and withdraw creative energy. The universe itself, originally a void of matterless space, experiences the touch of this subtle presence many times over vast cycles of time. The planets, whose beginnings were spewed from black holes as congealed bits of crystallized elements, are themselves the effect of a primal vibration wielded by this unseen Seer. From this original impetus manifests a series of reactions which, on the physical level, causes elements to chemically interact and congeal. The movement of these solid masses create the phenomena of a universe of name and form, swimming endlessly in a formless ocean of infinite space and set against the backdrop of a gradual and ultimately illu-

sory march of time. Essentially then, and as amazing as
it seems, space is capable of condensing into matter. A
matterless void, by some unknown and unseen cause,
proceeds to impregnate itself, filling boundless space
with bodies in motion. What is more, as recent scientific
discoveries suggest, matter also dissolves or gets
absorbed by encountering space. This occurs when a
mega black hole consisting of many micro black holes
collides with or encounters an astronomical body which
then disappears entirely.

In the conch shell is stored a miniature of this phe-
nomenon. It reflects the cosmic plan while simultaneously intimating the architect of this grand design. Its
outer shell represents the gross universe of name and
form consisting of the five elements while the space sur-
rounding it on all sides indicates the trackless void.
Within it lies the "inner space," formless yet humming
with the potential for manifestation. The gross universe,
then, is superimposed over a subtle Reality which has
given birth to vibrating matter and provided it with the
pervasive backdrop of space and time. In the language of
the Srimad Bhagavatam as told by Sri Krishna, *"Behold
this universe as spread out in the self and behold the self as
resting in me."* Thus, the conch shell reveals that form
and formlessness are interactive principles of one eternal
existence, Itself consciously intelligent and pure and perfect by nature. Further, that this pure and intelligent
Consciousness enters into the universe and animates
material shapes and forms is obvious. Knowing it in its
essential nature is a matter of direct experience rather
than explanation, but the Universal Mother's Conch provides powerful inspiration towards that end.

Mention has been made earlier of *bindu, nada, kalatita* — the initial seed, the primordial sound, and the web of time. Discussed in various ways throughout the six orthodox systems of Eastern Philosophy, these three correspond well with time, space, and causation. The universe depends upon and assumes its appearance of reality due to these three principles, which are strands that weave the tapestry over which the play of life and death — the sport of Consciousness — gets enacted. Evolution is impossible without them. If they are proved to be unreal then the entire universe must also be seen as an illusion. Such is the assertion of the theory of the unreality of the universe, for its process proceeds due to cause and effect played out over repetitious spans of time permeated by continual flux and change.

Proving the play of the universe to be unreal based upon action and reaction and perpetual motion is an important revelation. This step, however, does not actually prove to be an ultimate negation. Logically speaking, a universe of name and form, constantly in motion, can only be perceived as moving if there is a stationary witness to observe its movement. Name and form can only persist if there is a nameless, formless Reality that forms the ground for their existence in time and space. Time, space, and causality too, can only be perceived as long as there is a conscious, intelligent entity present to cognise and affirm their existence. Finally, initial vibration, which gives rise to all successive vibrations, can only be set in motion, given its power to vibrate, and defined as a motion called vibration by a stationary Reality. It is this Reality which the conch shell infers, the nature of which escapes detection, defies description, and thwarts all attempts to be known by anything outside Itself. Thus we are lead to the spiritual nature of Reality by the conch shell's explicit symbology.

In order that the conch shell's peal of exhilarating sound be heard, there must be one who initiates it. For there to be a creation, springing from the primal vibration, there must be a Creator who plants the initial seed, strikes the first note and sets the profuse waves in motion. An effect must have a cause, the universe must have an origin. The idea of a void cannot exist without the idea of filling it, and again, the act of filling infinite space with elements, planets, creatures, and intelligence that creates, inhabits, and defines a living universe, cannot be possible without a void to fill. The sacred conch shell, the perfect instrument to illustrate the homogenous blending of form and formlessness, rests in one of the Divine Mother's upraised hands, awaiting Her sweet Will. If She intends to raise it to Her blessed lips, the universe of name and form will explode into being. In this way will She activate the divine sport called the *Mahalila* — the play of Consciousness — intelligent Awareness expressing itself throughout the boundless universe. Though Consciousness will express through waves of multiplicity, in the end only uniformity will reign, existing as the substratum for all phenomenal existence. For God is the Ultimate Reality and the universe is merely a reflection. The dreamer still exists after waking but the dream fades and is forgotten. The sacred conch is the instrument that epitomizes subtle existence and gross manifestation, but the Mother Herself wields it as one of Her pervasive powers. As Ramprasad Sen, the poet/saint of India has said, *"The magician alone is real, his tricks are illusory."*

The Discus of Absolute Perfection

The Divine Mother's Discus, or *chakra*, forming an exact circle, represents perfection. This integral perfection is not a distant, transcendent and unreachable goal. It is a perpetual and ideal Truth which is ever-present despite all misconceptions, superimpositions and distortions, including the strictures of relativity and the projections of limited consciousness. Nor is its ideal nature limited only to transcendent or immediate conditions. The universe — the realm of becoming — is also included in its sweeping expanse.

To call the universe perfect would be, to some, a rash statement. To others, labeling it imperfect would be no less careless for, in fact, by design it is exactly as it is intended to be — it is perfect in its imperfection. Set up to facilitate multi-million year cycles, it is impeccably styled to accommodate the points of conscious light that inhabit it. These sparks of awareness possessed of body, mind and senses, resembling actors and actresses on a vast stage, undergo a thorough training in the lessons of individual existence in the universe. Like the *chakra*, which contains everything within its sleek circular shape, embodied beings possess an abundance of resources and abilities for their journey through space and time. The Supreme Being has provided them with their full share of perfection, though they often choose to forget or overlook it. Like the discus, whose circle and cycle is eternal, whose perfection is part of its design, the true nature of human beings is complete and all-abiding. Though their flesh, blood, and bone bodies may appear, rise, fall, and disappear, the stainless consciousness dwelling within them remains constant, shedding limited material structures as surely as a snake sheds its skin or a child dons and removes clothes. The birth, life, and death of these sheaths of matter are of relative significance compared to the birthless, deathless, eternally pure spark of conscious awareness that they carry. Yet even the sheaths reflect the permanence of the inner essence. Built of minute, eternal particles which are perpetually animate and full of deathless force, material shapes and forms merely rearrange to accommodate the expressive sport of pure Awareness, Itself indivisible and boundless, homogenous and infinite.

The entire scheme, created and placed in motion by a Master Intelligence informed by Truth Itself, is an error-free, mistake-proof, accident-immune condition, devoid also of chance or coincidence. Even the most pervasive ignorance resulting in the greatest misery and suffering only serves to gradually reveal an important secret of creation — that duality is inherent in the universal plan. This revelation in turn gives way to the innermost secret — that diversity springs from unity, that fragmentation is only apparent, that Consciousness is seamless and self-contained. Knowing the nature of Consciousness to be such, divine sport in the mode of absolute freedom proceeds unhindered. This, then, is the further symbology behind the Universal Mother's Discus — that its perfection is based upon Truth and Freedom.

As the Universal Mother's divine weapon, the discus is swift and immediate. It delivers its intended blow with ease and efficiency. Its aerodynamic design allows it to be an instrument of least resistance as it cuts through the dense materials of relativity and illusion without delay. Nor can its keen edge be dulled in the least, for its circular motion and unique shape hone and sharpen perpetually. Thus, the chakra and its description illustrate the power of Truth perfectly, for it is lightning fast, impossible to divert, perpetually keen, and minutely exact. Freedom, which is gained by strict adherence to the Truth, is also represented well by the discus. Its flight, like the experience of true freedom, is meaningful, exalted, and unimpeded. When its target is destroyed, it returns to the source of its power — the Universal Mother. Freedom too, when the imposition of bondage is removed, expresses itself through the boundless Grace of the Absolute, its eternal origin.

The Divine Mother, Sri Durga, values this powerful weapon exceedingly, reserving it for the destruction of the most tenacious ignorance. The discus is also representative of omniscience, for on the field of battle, amidst confusing chaos, the discus acts as Mother's weapon of scrutiny as it soars above the conflagration, destroying and observing alternately while returning to its wielder for communion and direction. Therefore does the symbology of the discus become complete, for knowledge proceeds by observation and experience, and when properly informed and guided, reflects Truth. Truth, in turn, as has been mentioned, allows for freedom which in turn brings true peace, unalloyed bliss, and lasting happiness.

The Divine Mala of Spiritual Intensity

Whereas the sword and discus are weapons of action and dynamism, the Divine Mother's Mala, much like the conch, symbolizes an abiding and subtle principle — that of abiding Truth and spiritual growth. The fragrant and beautiful rosary which adorns one hand of Sri Durga primarily signifies the existence and dissemination of the spiritual sciences such as *japa*, chanting of the holy names, prayer, meditation, and all other forms of worship. This auspicious tool is invaluable and represents almost every facet of spiritual life. As a tool for discipline and transmission, it symbolizes the precious art of concentration by which the attainment of happiness, balance and peace of mind are acquired. In this application, the practice of japa is of utmost importance. The ability to harness the power of thought and focus the mind with single-minded concentration is acquired through this spiritual art form. This is accomplished with the aid of the sacred seed syllables called *bija mantras*, and utilization of the divine names which accompany the turning of the beads. By constant repetition of these powerful influences, a calm and centered state of mind is attained through which the aspirant can proceed onward to deeper internal experiences such as insight and meditation. Prayer and devotions, the mainstay of worship, are also made more effective by this discipline, for the attention of the Divine Being is drawn towards those devotees who invoke the holy names and who strive to uncover the intrinsic spark of divinity abiding within. Thus does intimate communion with the blessed Lord and Divine Mother of the Universe become possible.

Relative to concentration, the mala, or rosary, is also a symbol of the Mother's prodigious memory, for not only does it signify the recitation of innumerable holy names and sacred mantras, it also implies the abiding existence of the powerful and infinite abundance of divine wisdom* contained within the religious and philosophical traditions of the world. Like its counterpart, the conch shell, the mala also represents sound, sound symbol, meaning and manifestation. Whereas the conch shell reflects these principles through an elemental perspective associated with creation, preservation, and destruction, the mala is inherently involved with the representation of eternal knowledge and the transmission of it through powerful wisdom streams. These flows of subtle intelligence are eternally existent but must have avenues of expression through which to cascade down into human consciousness. The japa mala signifies access to these precious teachings and also serves as a mouthpiece for their transmission.

Following this line of thinking, the radiant rosary points to the connection between the teaching and the taught — the teacher, or *guru*. That the Divine Mother is holding the mala indicates Her unsurpassed qualification at bestowing initiation and teachings to and through all spiritual preceptors, thereby granting the will to perform *sadhana* for the attainment of emancipation leading to total absorption into Absolute Reality. The mala and the guru together symbolize the power of purification, transformation and transcendence, and thereby signify the dawning of enlightenment and realization.

Even these many profound qualities do not exhaust the japa mala's capacity. The blessed rosary also represents the means by which devotion is gleaned and granted. Therefore, it is a cherished instrument among the devotees of the path of *Bhakti*, or supreme love. Love for the divine name, love for the practice, devotion to the teacher, thirst for the teachings, and reverence for the source of wisdom who holds the sacred japa mala — the blessed rosary is holiness itself. It trains and allows the mind to rest upon God in one-pointed concentration. What is more, it causes the mind to ascend to a condition beyond the drudgery of systematic practice, for it transforms the idea of "becoming" into the reality of pure Being. This is accomplished in stages. The practice of japa with the mala first confers protection. It then facilitates remembrance and concentration. Finally, it results in the experience of bliss as the power of the mantra and the holy name flood the receptive mind with feelings of joy and gratitude. Such a valuable tool should be used to full advantage by those who would discover and realize the true meaning for human existence.

The Bell of Crystalline Clarity

Sri Durga's powerful Bell of Clarity causes instantaneous insight to manifest in the minds of those who seek spiritual awakening. This special article signals the arrival of auspicious timing with regards to enlightenment. Those who are fortunate enough to feel its healing vibration as it penetrates into the innermost depths of their being, realize an end to ignorance and delusion and discover an infinite expanse of sublime experience.

The sacred bell has also been described as an awesome weapon, for its sound strikes terror into the hearts of the negative forces *(asuras)* inhabiting human awareness, causing them to dissipate swiftly and completely. Wonderfully enough, this same intonation produces the most beneficial effect on the Divine Mother's devotees, manifesting as an intoxicating music which attracts them into an ecstasy of internal delight.

On a universal or cosmic level, the Divine Mother can bring immediate silence to Her entire collection of worlds and to all levels of existence — physical, vital, mental and spiritual. This is because the bell represents the power of pure sound or logos, the *anahata dhvani*, from which the entire creation has proceeded. This root sound which emanates from Her divine article further manifests as all sciences, sacred or secular, manifested by thought, written or spoken, or expressed in any way. Additionally, the all-important quality of communication as well as the arts of music, art, poetry, and motion all are represented by Her bell of absolute clarity. One shake of this instrument is sufficient to remove all delusions or impositions from Reality and cause sentient beings to become absorbed in the contemplation of their eternal nature called the *Atman.* Ramprasad Sen, the devoted child of the Universal Mother, describes this awe-inspiring phenomena:

"The Supreme Lady moves with dramatic stride and brilliant smile. Like the vast thunder at the final dissolution of the universe, Her cry of Truth sounds forth — Stop! Stop! Cease and be still!...Directly She advances to the stronghold of the enemy and stares down death with Her ferocious eyes. This poet trembles at Her astonishing epiphany and sings tremulously: 'The realm of being born and dying is immersed in ceaseless war. Death is constantly attacking with superior forces. I cannot resist its over-whelming illusion. My Warrior Mother alone can save me.'"

So many precious shades of meaning are associated with the Universal Mother's divine articles that it becomes impossible to express them all. The infinite expanse of Her creation, from lower worlds to angelic regions and beyond, are all filled with sacred symbology. The Bell of Absolute Clarity is no exception to this rule of infinite expression. Effective on a cosmic level as a weapon in the hands of the Supreme Goddess, it also proves efficacious on a subtle level within the realm of devotional worship. Here, it is found in the hands of the worshipper who sits before the altar invoking the presence of divinity in all things.   As a constant drone or a single stroke, its implementation in sacred ritual prompts the same instantaneous response from the minds of the devout, who thrill to the audible appearance of incarnate blessings flowing from its vibrating surface.   Thus does the sacred bell represent an all-pervasive clarity associated with spiritual awakening on all levels of existence. Whether wielded as an awesome weapon by the Universal Mother on the battlefield of relativity or intoned gently in adoration of the sublime presence of Divinity during sacred worship *(puja/arati)*, its function is universal and the result is beneficial and healing.

It is obvious that the conch, mala, and bell all share similar qualities with regards to sound.   This again points to one of the Universal Mother's supreme secrets — that vibration is the keynote to the mystery of creation.   The conch, whose sound vibration is inherent in its design, represents that part of the creative process that is associated with the components of nature *(prakriti)*, the building blocks of the universal structure.   The mala, with regards to sound, represents the expressive aspect of sound associated with knowledge and its dissemination, particularly the wisdom that is essential and eternal and which concerns spiritual growth.   The sacred bell reflects sound as the penetrating force of integral insight that stills the conflagration of chaotic forces and brings immediate concentration and peaceful absorption into Absolute Reality.   Thus, following this theme, and in keeping with Eastern cosmology, the conch could represent creation, the mala, preservation, and the bell, dissolution.   In addition, the conch represents the Immanent or what is visible, the mala represents the Transcendent or what is subtle or unseen, and the bell represents the Absolute or what is known by direct perception. These functions or representations are not necessarily distinct or separate, for each of the three reflect and contain the power of each of the others. This can be understood by taking the Divine Trinity into account and briefly describing their respective functions.

The Divine Trinity, Brahma, Vishnu and Shiva, act as both anthropomorphic gods and cosmological principles. That is, they are beings endowed with name and form existing in supersensual realms who also manifest as formless dynamic energy to perform the functions associated with the laws of the universe. As emanations of Ishvara, they contain both their own essence and their own expressive power *(Shakti)*. As congealed conscious Light they illumine the worlds with their radiance, appearing in sacred vision to their votaries, while their Shakti power permeates all realms of existence as irrepressible animating force. The two aspects are essentially inseparable, and so too are their respective functions. Brahma, the power of creation, cannot create unless old structures are destroyed, therefore He is reliant on Shiva, the God of dissolution. Furthermore, what Brahma creates retains its lasting power from Vishnu who preserves and perpetuates the cosmic flow. Both Vishnu and Shiva depend upon Brahma for the appearance of the three worlds, otherwise there would be nothing to preserve or dissolve. In this way, one can infer an intrinsic interconnectedness and interdependence between the three.

However, each aspect of divinity contains the ability to support the power of the other two. For instance,

Brahma preserves as well, for He maintains an ongoing protection over and spontaneous recitation of the four Vedas perpetually. Vishnu creates and destroys, as many a god *(sura)* and demon *(asura)* can attest to, for He once granted Brahma the power to create by destroying the two demons, Madhu and Kaitabha, who were formed from bits of wax that dropped from His ears while He was plunged in cosmic sleep before the interminable creative cycle began. Shiva too, creates and preserves, for His destructive power leaves the field of potential manifestation free and clear for constructive expression, and He presides over this new energy by fostering the spiritual growth of the devotees through the dissemination of spiritual wisdom. In this way do the universal laws interweave and overlap, and similar to this also do the respective functions of the conch, mala and bell share their inherent properties and qualities.

Regarding the Divine Mother Durga's application of these tools in battle, and indicative of the amazing effect that they produce on negative forces, the *Srimad Devi Bhagavatam* makes mention of their appearance:

"The great demon general, Chiksura, departed for battle, mounted on his chariot and accompanied by his own army. The powerful Tamra accompanied him as his attendant. The sky and all the quarters became filled with the clamor of their vast army. The auspicious Devi Bhagavati saw them before Her and She made an extraordinarily wonderful sound with Her Conch shell, with Her Bowstring, and with Her great Bell. The Asuras heard that and trembled and fled, crying and speaking amongst each other in fear."

With references like these, a great world scripture gives validity and emphasis to the superior forces that gather on the side of ultimate good, removing the impositions of egotism, the existence of doubt, and the illusion of death forever.

The Winecup of Divine Essence

The Universal Mother manifests as the animating power of life called vital force *(prana)* and the primal Consciousness which ultimately supports it as well. For this reason She holds aloft the Winecup of Divine Essence. This indicates that the Divine Mother Herself is the very lifeblood of the universe and its eternal foundation. That She Herself drinks from the vessel implies that all beings have their life forces merged in Her and live in Her. Few concerns of the Divine Mother are more important to Her than the nurturing of every precious spark of Awareness which are parts of Her own Being. The principles of origin, sustenance, and immersion are therefore perfectly demonstrated in the symbology reflected by the winecup.

Both vital force *(prana)* and Consciousness *(chaitanya)*, are indivisible. Prana, however, is limited to the physical universe and the heavenly regions whereas Consciousness is all-pervasive and infinite by nature. Pure Consciousness and its dynamic power called *Shakti* constitute the living awareness which saturates existence and appears as the intelligence inherent in living beings. The two are one in essence, are timeless, deathless and without beginning. Prana permeates nature *(prakriti)* and animates the sentient forms and structures created from its materials, entering into them and operating them through its various salubrious movements and flows *(prana, apana, samana, udana, and vyana)*. The *Prasnopanishad* describes prana as the chief function within the created worlds, for it holds and supports the bodies of all beings. Asked who is the greatest among the universal functions (gods), Pippalada, the great Rishi, answers, *"The ether, air, fire, water, earth, speech, mind, eye, and ear, each of these manifest their power, vaunt, and say, 'We, each of us, holding the body, support it.'"* Prana then intervenes and claims its sovereignty over them as the very life force animating them all. They do not believe the prana so it demonstrates its power:

"He from indignation appeared to go out upwards from the body; thereupon as he was about to go out, all others seemed to go out, and when he was established, all others were also established. Just as bees go out when their Queen goes out, and settle down when she settles down, so did the speech, mind, eye, ears, etc., do the same. Being satisfied they praised the prana."

The Winecup of Divine Essence, then, symbolizes life force and conscious awareness — indivisible essences in relative and absolute modes. These are both unseen subtle principles responsible for the manifestation and animation of the world of name and form. The Divine Mother, the holder of the sacred chalice, reveals that the Supreme Being — an independent, self-existent Divine Reality — is the source of life and existence and the creator and preserver of all its various expressions. That She drinks the essential elixir of life and its conscious force from the holy cup indicates that both life force and conscious awareness originate in Her, proceed from Her, manifest through individual structures apparently separate from Her, and return to and get absorbed in Her. It is a grand design revealing the oneness of all existence, whether external, internal or transcendent.

Another important facet clearly reflected through the symbol of the winecup is the principle of satisfaction and fulfillment. The two aspects pertinent to this inscrutable area of life are needs and desires. The energy associated with each is of a different nature. What we require to satisfy the necessities of daily living and perpetuate our lives is essential, whereas those extraneous things we seek after for pleasure and excitement are nonessential. The former allows for the maintenance of our bodies and minds so that growth and progress can occur while the latter, more often than not, dissipates the energy received from day to day sustenance and creates repercussive situations that result in conditions of obsession, attachment and bondage.

With regards to desire, another distinction can be pointed out. Those whose motives are based upon individual gratification and characterized by selfish preoccupations and inordinate clinging to sensual pursuits continue to expand their mind's appetite for more and similar gratification. This creates a vortex of conflicting energies *(karma)* primed for retribution and amasses a huge store of inherited tendencies *(samskaras)*. Trying to placate the mind's erratic energies by indulging in desires through sensual experience is futile. This has been likened to pouring gas on a fire in order to extinguish it. In contrast, those beings who attain self-surrender to the higher will of the Supreme Being and offer the small fires of individual desire into the blazing bonfire of consummate knowledge have their karmas burnt away, *"like a heap of cotton in fire,"* and attain freedom from attachment and craving. This results in ultimate satisfaction and abiding happiness, like the refuge that cool waters afford from the heat of the midday sun.

She who sustains the entire creation also liberates it. To receive the boon of spiritual emancipation and break free from the imaginary bondage of earthly attachment and selfish grasping is to imbibe the nectar of immortality. Those who would drink from the Mother's Winecup of satiety and fulfillment discover a twofold delight. First, all desires get ultimately satisfied and vanish in a single lifetime and, second, all noble expectations reach fruition according to the guidance of the Supreme Will. In this way, a draught taken from the Mother's sacred chalice is transformative, but only those who are possessed of inner strength and daring will draw from its contents.

The function of a cup is to get filled and emptied in turns. The Supreme Goddess fills us with noble aspirations but these are blended with our limited desires and misguided expectations. Through the working out of karma over many lifetimes, the aspiring soul (mind) begins to recognize the difference between desire and virtue, insight and delusion, reality and illusion. Truth stands clearly revealed when external forms and projections are perceived to be ephemeral by nature. The principle of the winecup, then, operates through the granting of boons based upon the exposure and destruction of all that is small and mean in human nature. This extremely beneficial trade-off allows a distillation and refinement of human consciousness that teaches one of the more essential lessons of spiritual growth — mature renunciation. The winecup is also seen as a vessel from which the Divine Mother drinks the blood of Her vanquished foes, the negative forces which oppose Her superior position of unbounded freedom and cling to their own distorted desire for individual power. Such poisonous tendencies She steeps over the fire of knowledge and converts into a heady mash which She then consumes heartily. In this way, Her auspicious winecup acts as a device for saving the universe from detrimental negativities that could threaten the very foundation of universal harmony. The winecup, then, like the sword, reveals itself as weapon as well as healer.

The Shield of Complete Protection

The universe depends on the flawless protection of the Divine Mother and where Her spiritual children are concerned, Her intense scrutiny of all matters is comprehensive and far-seeing. In this way, Mother Durga's Shield of Complete Protection reveals the relation between the power of protection and ability of foresight. Advance knowledge and proper planning are interdependent partners in the struggle for success or victory. Neither of these are attainable or effective without the power of deflection which the Universal Mother's powerful shield offers. Her shield provides a pervasive and impenetrable barrier of ultimate protection which She uses like a seasoned warrior. Therefore, the above mentioned attributes are all interconnected qualities that form an integral part of the shield's powerful aura. Together they deter negative forces from gaining a foothold in the often precarious domain of human consciousness.

The shield protects every speck of consciousness that inhabits Her vast planetary realms. In addition to protection, other forces are present and at work as well. Attributes such as compassion and concern are also facets of the shield's unique and comprehensive design and reflect the Universal Mother's boundless love for all creatures. Her love is all-containing, for She protects the helpless and simultaneously accepts all of the intense abuse showered upon Her by the negative forces. Here the perfection of the Divine Mother is seen in all its glory. Love, compassion and protection are all based upon sacrifice. The shield takes the endless abuse of countless blows upon its surface, yet yields not and complains not. The Divine Mother also accepts the scars and trials of war, but remains impervious to them, staying focused upon protecting the lives of Her children. She has become Her articles of war. She acts as a shield for the universe, which indicates Her perfect and complete sacrifice and willingness to accept the suffering of all beings who take refuge in Her.

Looking deep into the mystery of the Divine Mother and Her shield, an enthralling and sobering vision appears. As the poet/saint Ramprasad sings, the blood of sacrifice from numerous wounds streams down Her radiant form *"as red flowers float on dark waters."* She willingly takes upon Herself the suffering of the entire creation, yet Her compassion for all beings, good or evil, continues to remain intact. Her compassion is so far-reaching that She even confers boons of refuge upon the *asuras* (demons) who oppose and assail Her. Even these wayward beings possess Her gift of pure Awareness somewhere in their being, though it is clouded over by distorted passions. Being inflated with pride and driven by greed, they expend all their energies in vain pursuits, all for the wrong reasons. Eventually they find Her power irresistible, and fall at Her feet of protection, awaiting the final transforming blow from Her Sword of Wisdom. These hapless beings represent the many evil thoughts, misguided intentions, negative actions and other discrepancies perpetrated by all creatures inhabiting the realms where cause and effect hold sway. Other beings, though they are not evil by nature, are nevertheless deluded and commit negative actions out of ignorance. These two kinds of deluded beings manifest two similar kinds of threats to the Mother's universe. With the unknowing ones, She receives their acts born of ignorance on Her shining armor, reflecting a portion of the effects back onto the perpetrators as valuable lessons while simultaneously protecting them from the most detrimental repercussions. Acts of wanton cruelty committed by those of malicious intent She bears on Her own person, destroying their poisonous wrath with characteristic detachment and finally transforming the vicious assailants with the purity of Her own blood sacrifice.

Therefore, even evil demons become Her devoted servants and have their karmas and imperfections wiped away. Through these miraculous events can be seen the evolutionary process of creation, preservation, and destruction, the subtle principle of transmutation of energy, and the ascension of all beings to perfection. This epitomizes the triumph of good over evil and the transmigrating soul's arrival at transcendence leading to union with the Supreme Self. The purport, purpose, and perfection of the cosmic plan becomes visible through the Universal Mother's adamant resolve to protect Her creation. Her love indeed knows no bounds! Without this quality of protection, chaos would reign supreme in the universe. What is more, its presence in the cosmic scheme provides proof of God's existence. Her shield is at work eternally, whether seen or unobserved, throughout every moment of every life. It is no wonder that Her devotees sing, *Jai Mahamayi ki Jai!* Victory abides with the Divine Mother of the Universe!

The Bow of Unerring Projection
& Flawless Concentration

The Divine Mother's sacred Bow of Unerring Projection holds a special place in the arsenal of the Her extraordinary powers. Indeed, its presence makes itself known in many of the fascinating stories that fill the pages of the holy scriptures of India. Especially in the *Itihasa*, the spiritually oriented historical accounts, do we find it appearing in various contexts and situations. The legendary bows of Sri Ram, Sri Krishna and Lord Shiva, to name a few, have played a significant role in the famous battles that have challenged these time-honored divine heroes. Their epic struggles and victories occupy entire chapters of the great *Ramayana*, the *Mahabharata*, and the *Srimad Bhagavatam*.

In this respect, the Divine Mother's powerful bow is also well-known and revered. The awesome battles which the Universal Mother undertakes for the good of the world are always attended by showers of arrows so thick that they darken the sky over the battlefield. The speed and dexterity with which She operates Her bow is baffling to the eye, and many a demonic force has had ample reason to fear both Her concentration and Her accuracy. Even well before She decides to fill the sky with clouds of arrows, She strikes Her bowstring with such force that the sound reverberates over the entire battlefield, sending thrills of fear and anguish into the hearts of Her enemies. The *Srimad Devi Bhagavatam* contains many accounts of these heroics:

"*The Devi blew Her Conch shell so loud that the ten quarters of the sky reverberated; in the meantime, the powerful lion on which She rode became angry and roared ferociously. Hearing that sound, the Gods, Munis, Yaksas, Siddhas, and Kinnaras became very glad. A dreadful fight then ensued between Chandika Devi and the two demons Chanda and Munda with arrows, axes, and other weapons, causing terror to the weak. The Chandika Devi became very wrathful and cut to pieces all the arrows shot by their opposing armies, hurling in turn arrows serpentlike upon them. Taking Her mighty Bow, the Devi shot so many arrows that the battle ground seemed overcast with arrows just as the clouds get covered over with locusts, dreadful to the cultivators.*"

In these awe-inspiring accounts of the Universal Mother's prowess are thus found abundant symbologies. Relative to the sacred bow, it can be said that the Mother's marvelous and stunning appearance on the field of battle is heralded by the cloud of arrows overhead, all shot from this awesome weapon. In this sense, the bow symbolizes the Supreme Will which is the initial cause representing both origin and projection. In the mode of action, the Mother draws forth the bow before any other weapon, and thus signals the approach of all that is destructive to the negative forces and all that is auspicious to Her creation. Since it is a weapon for distance warfare rather than close contact fighting, it is aptly suited to announce Her arrival on the scene. This has cosmic connotations as well.

The subtle ramifications of the bow's existence and function can be easily associated with the triple aspect of the cosmic process — creation, preservation and destruction. When the Mother of the Universe wants to give birth to the creation She spontaneously empowers the forces of projection and appearance simultaneously, for the two work in conjunction. Thus She gives birth to the world of name and form by sending forth Her power *(sristhi)* and maintaining what it manifests *(stithi)*. The bow, then, contains both the potential for the manifestation of Her power and the ability to carry it out. It is also able to project the power of destruction which eventually dissolves the world of name and form back into its primal origin *(pralaya)*.

Spiritually, these symbologies relate to the internal workings of awakening, self-effort, and purification, also related to creation, maintenance and dissolution. The bow signifies the approach of something powerful and sublime — an initial intuitive sensitivity which signals the first stirrings of higher values and insights within the human consciousness. As this tendency emerges it needs development, and here too the bow acts as an aid, representing the all-important power of concentration. As the emergence of inherent spirituality is recognized, the discrepancies present in the human mind become all the more obvious. The power of concentration allows for the destruction of these unwanted occupants resulting in the eventual and absolute purification of the mind. This facilitates the experiences associated with the direct spiritual perception of Divine Reality. Amidst the movement of this cohesive process, the powers contained within the bow shine forth as beneficial aids in the evolution of the transmigrating consciousness.

To hold the bow steady, to draw the bowstring with strength, to aim with concentrated attention at the target, to release at the proper moment — these and other fine points of archery combine to epitomize the essence of the art. In the same way, the spiritual aspirant must remain steady and persevere, must complete all activities with inner strength and resolve intact, must concentrate with one-pointed attention upon what is most important in life and remain focused despite the many distractions of the seductive world. Finally, the aspirant must remain alert and know when the proper time to renounce has arrived, for letting go of the mundane realm brings human awareness closer to its true Source, while remaining engrossed with worldly affairs only perpetuates more karmic repercussions. Those who desire unbounded freedom will utilize the powers represented by the sacred bow to attain immersion into Ultimate Reality — the goal and purpose of human life.

The Arrow of Inscrutable Accuracy

The Divine Mother's Arrow of Inscrutable Accuracy shares some similar properties with the bow in that it is also a weapon of projection. Whereas the bow epitomizes the power of projection, the arrow represents that which gets projected and how, when, and where it arrives. This all amounts to a comprehensive knowledge of detail and an unfailing knack for locating and penetrating into all levels of operation, whether they be universal functions, subtle occurrences, primordial secrets, or even the thick, multilayered realm of actions and reactions.

In this latter area, the Mother attends to such things as how cause and effect — the actions and repercussions sown and reaped by human beings — get worked out. This is accomplished exactingly by the Divine Mother, for Her arrows of insight, like the cloud of arrows darkening the sky over the battlefield, rain down thick upon the field of human actions, discovering, fulfilling, and granting just retribution for every one of them. Right timing also plays an important role in this sweeping task. Beings experience gathering the fruits of their actions and learn the lessons pertinent to their lives according to a meticulous foresight and insight present within the Universal Mother. In this way the arrow shows its connection as an agent of destiny, both lesser and larger. Matters small and numerous do not escape its detection yet major affairs connected with important issues such as life, relationships, spiritual growth and death are equally and effectively dealt with. Time, clime, and circumstance — nothing escapes the thorough scrutiny of Mother's shower of arrows. This comprehensive inspection, at once spontaneous and far-reaching, is an eternal trademark of the Divine Mother of the Universe as pure *Shakti*.

That the Divine Mother is holding an individual arrow in one of Her hands indicates Her mastery over all matters in the universe, even the most infinitesimal. The Mother's pervasive scrutiny of the realm of time, space and causation reveals the arrow as an instrument of omniscience whose streamlined shape allows it to find and penetrate into the smallest opening. In this regard, it can discover and enter into the slightest defect in the armor of negativity as well, destroying the most secret and best laid plans of the *asuras* and other demonic forces that plot for control and supremacy over the realm of name and form.

The Arrow of Accuracy is equally effective in the realms of human ignorance and egotism, that narrow aspect of consciousness which gives birth to such negative impulses and allows them to grow. The small, seemingly insignificant arrow, manifesting as the movement of positive insight within the human mind, notes the presence of such evil and waits for the proper time to rain a flood of destruction down upon it. This ruins the most secret and best laid plans of the asuras and other demonic forces that plot for control and supremacy over the world of name and form. Ramprasad, the poet/saint of India, describes the dynamic interaction of the Universal Mother and Her healing powers within the heart and mind of the devotee:

> *"Awakened souls rush towards Her fragrant Lips like bees drawn by red blossoms. She is the flower of timeless awareness — ever young, naked, thrilling to behold. Yet She wields Her Sword of Truth as a seasoned warrior. Volleys of arrows from Her Bow of insight pierce the very heart of selfish clinging...."* [8]

Another important characteristic of the arrow is that it buries itself deep into its target. This suggests not only its power of penetration as listed in several ways above, but also reflects the essential truth of oneness or unity. That its flight is straight, swift, and exact relates to growth and evolution — the realm of becoming — but its penetration into its intended target demonstrates absorption into the realm of pure Being. When both aspects are taken into consideration, the full significance of the arrow gets revealed. It originates from the Mother's Bow — Her weapon of Divine Intent. It assumes its sure and direct flight on Her command for the purpose of bringing insight into the human mind through the destruction of ignorance and evil. Finally, it enters into and becomes one with the object of its directive and remains buried there, at rest, with its impetus dissolved, releasing its healing power. Thus does it reveal transcendence, transformation and immanence; unity, manifestation and diversity; nondual, qualified, and dual modes, all to be components of one Absolute Reality. As the Vedantic lore proclaims:

> *"What is visible is Infinite. What is invisible is also Infinite. From the Infinite the finite has come, but being Infinite, only Infinite remains."* [9]

The Spear of Deep Penetration

The Spear of Deep Penetration, which Sri Durga holds, epitomizes the power of penetration into the stronghold of negativity — an ability at which She is extremely adept and perfectly suited for. Like the arrow, the spear is an important weapon for both offense and defense. Therefore, the wielder of it assumes the responsibility for the outcome of crucial matters with regards to life, growth, and death. In the case of the Divine Mother, that She holds the spear reveals Her as the Supreme *Karma Yogini* — the ultimate agent of all action and the director of its outcome. The appearance of such powerful articles as the discus, spear, sword, bow, and shield also reveals Her as the creator, projector, sustainer, protector, and destroyer of phenomenal existence.

In traditional iconography, the Bhagavati Durga Devi is shown with Her spear in the heart of the demon, *Mahisasura,* while She rides astride the lion. Therefore, it is clear that the main purpose for the Mother's incarnation as Sri Durga is to subdue and vanquish the demonic forces that oppose divine rule and threaten human life. That Her weapon is in the very heart of Her foe is indicative that She possesses the extensive force to penetrate into the most powerful stronghold of evil and accomplish a task which no other, not even the gods Brahma, Vishnu,

Shiva, are able to deal with. The pervasive and persistent powers of negativity die hard in the firmament of human consciousness. A stroke of Mother's Wisdom Sword or a fatal stab with Her Spear of Deep Penetration — both weapons of serious warfare — suffice to eradicate every trace of such influence from the human mind.

Sri Durga's familiar pose atop the king of beasts indicates that She has complete control and mastery over the senses and their objects of enjoyments. This serves to transmit the lesson to mankind that to live a balanced life and attain fulfillment, one must keep desires and animal passions under control. The Mother, Her mount, Her spear and the demon, form one unbroken image in singular cohesive motion. The Mother hereby shows through example how desires and passions breed negativity, which in turn are overcome by rising above them by utilizing self-effort, self-surrender, and reliance upon Her Grace. Poised above this foursome are the other divine articles such as the winecup, mala, bell, and conch. Thus, when the business of encountering and neutralizing negative forces within the mind is accomplished, higher and more refined avenues of expression and realization await.

In the area of spiritual growth, the spear signifies penetration of a more subtle nature. Its design implies a deep insight into the secrets of the universe and knowledge of the essential teachings of the scriptures. These both reflect the existence of a sublime condition beyond the universe. In this regard, the spear brings to mind the Mother's servants who disseminate the teachings and transmit the inner meanings inherent in them. The guru, then, is the instrument which the Mother uses to plunge deep into the heart and mind of the aspirant, installing and instilling the devotional wisdom teachings there. When the tool is withdrawn upon completing this service, the internal awareness of the disciple has been sewn with the seeds of future realization. The disciple must cultivate and water the internal field of consciousness in a resolved and committed manner. During this process, the spear resumes its role as defender of the field until the aspirant gains illumination and acquires his or her own divine weapons.

Meditations

The Divine Articles as Methods for Meditation

Throughout this study of the *Ten Divine Articles of Sri Durga*, rich symbologies have been utilized to convey a sense of the subtle presence of the Universal Mother and to explain Her many powers, activities, and occupations. With these in mind, it is now possible to give a guided meditation on each of Her powerful weapons. In this way, our minds can derive benefits from internal contemplative disciplines and we can implement these into our daily life to insure and maintain a stable spiritual growth.

To begin, sit in a comfortable but alert fashion with back straight and breath regulated. This will slow the beating of the heart and calm the thought waves of the mind. Excessive shifting of posture and recourse to various breathing exercises should be avoided, as these tend to identify consciousness with the body and can cause the mind to become imbalanced. One posture (half-lotus or full lotus) and a natural, slow and deliberate in and out breath are the mainstays of spiritual practice. A spiritual orientation rather than a physical one is the reason that a true aspirant takes recourse to purificatory practices. If worldly considerations and purely physical practices are mixed in with our *sadhana* (spiritual discipline) they will distract our minds and direct them back towards earthly desires and attachments. If this be the case, we might as well return to the pursuit of terrestrial pleasures and possessions and give up higher aspirations. Therefore, make a right resolve in this matter from the outset and refuse to compromise.

Since the purpose of life is to realize God, and God is the Reality without a second who is ever-present, infinite, and the essence of our innermost being, a personal relationship must be cultivated. For this purpose, the paths of love and understanding are the most suitable ways of quickly realizing Divine Reality. If you have been initiated into the secrets of spiritual life by a guru and possess the auspicious gift of a mantra, you can achieve a peaceful state of mind swiftly and without danger by beginning your meditation with *japa*, the perfect devotional exercise. If not, you may chant *Om* audibly a few times and then concentrate upon this sacred word until the mind becomes still. Repeating a holy name and concentrating on a divine form can also be effective.

In this meditation, we are focusing on the feminine aspect of Ultimate Reality. Essentially, God is beyond gender, but cannot be limited, even by formlessness. Absolute Reality appears as material substance, as consciousness associated with name and form, and as formless essence, in much the same way that water manifests in three conditions as solid (ice), liquid (water), or vapor (gas). In these three instances, it would be illogical to argue that H2O is not present in them all. Just so, God is present in matter as energy, in earthly and heavenly forms as sapient intelligence, and in formless Reality as pure Consciousness which pervades all three as well. That God pervades everything as Consciousness is an obvious fact, whether one cares to name It or not. Even insentient things have a sort of consciousness — a molecular structure that vibrates. It is best, therefore, to put the mind's doubts to rest on this issue and accept Divine Reality. Strive to perceive Its presence in all things, in all beings, in all circumstances. Swift progress will be the inevitable result.

With regards to "superior and inferior" modes of meditation upon Reality, some argue that formless meditation is superior, others, that meditating on God with form is higher. Both miss the point. When Divine Reality is seen to exist everywhere and in everything, all ideas and assumptions of what is higher and what is lower disappear and only God remains. This is the effective kind of meditation that matures the act of discrimination, transcends all thoughts of renunciation, and sees through the duality of bondage and liberation. As Gaudapada, the consummate *Advaitan* states, it removes the illusory line of demarcation between matter and Spirit, between creature and Creator, between mankind and God.

If you are one of those who doubts or dismisses the idea of Divine Reality, there is much room for growth and plenty to consider. Fish may be oblivious of the existence of water simply because they cannot see it, yet it surrounds them as the very support and foundation of their existence. In truth, they could not live without it. Do birds, flying through the sky, deny the existence of air simply because it remains invisible to their senses? Even if they tried, the wind would prove them wrong, and in doing so would continue to lift their wings higher, making their lives happier and easier. These analogies act to affirm the existence of an unseen Reality. Though they are conceived using examples in nature, this makes them all the more convincing, for even nature demonstrates the divine characteristic of infinity. The universe even by itself is proof of God's existence, for can there be a creation without a Creator? Logic and rationale again point to the Ultimate Truth. Therefore, for the atheist or agnostic, a rational pursuit of Truth must be undertaken using reasonable methods until these subtle revelations visit the mind.

With these main issues resolved in our minds, we can now enjoy the privilege of formal meditation, taking up each of the Universal Mother's Divine Articles in turn.

The Sword

Nondual Truth, Wisdom, Discrimination, Scrutiny, Purification, Perception, Transcendence, Enlightenment, Peace, and Freedom.

Establishing an attitude of surrender to the Universal Mother and concentrating upon the *Atman,* that part of every being which is perfect in essence, take up Her Sword of Wisdom and visualize it in the mind. Imagine this powerful weapon and concentrate on its intricate design, its sheen, its beauty, its eternal nature. Note the sacred Sanskrit runes carved into its surface and contemplate their significance. Attempt to grasp the pure and divine presence of the radiant Being who holds it aloft, poised to deal an all-transforming stroke of liberating perception. As you gaze upon Her radiant form, contemplate the sword's significance with these thoughts:

The Mother's Sword reveals Truth. Where it falls, delusion and illusion cease to exist. It fosters wisdom and destroys ignorance. It confers the necessary boon of discrimination and provides the heightened power of observation needed for life in the world. It grants purity to the mind, removing all impurities such as doubt, despair, depression and fear. It allows higher insights to rise to the surface of consciousness and facilitates the rare boon of transcendence which strengthens witness consciousness. It leaves the mind enlightened and free of all limitations and superimpositions, bringing true peace to bear. Finally, it leaves awareness pure and unencumbered, in whatever mode of existence it chooses to rest.

Mentally salute the Wisdom Sword and symbolically offer your mind to the Universal Mother along with all of its plans, intentions, thoughts, assumptions, concepts, imperfections, knowledge, and various other contents. Consciously receive the sword stroke across your neck, signifying the offering of the head and all the mind possesses to the Divine Mother of the Universe. Finish the meditation by remaining conscious of the detached mind, free from the body idea, bereft of any identification with name and form. Abide in that completely emancipated condition, floating above the relative plane of existence. Gradually become aware of the world of name and form, perceiving it as a radiant emanation of the Infinite Being. Observe and remember how insignificant all of the typical worries and concerns of the world appear when transported into such a high state of awareness. Bring this quality of refined awareness back into the body and consciously radiate it to all sentient and insentient beings occupying the realm of time, space, and causation. Again, humbly and reverently salute the Divine Mother of the Universe and resolve to execute Her Will in all matters.

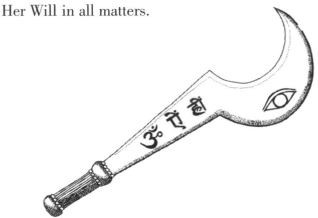

The Conch

Auspiciousness, Victory, Peace, Harmony, Unity,
Creation, Preservation, Dissolution, Divine Inference.

Concentrating upon Sri Durga as a divine image in
the mind, picture Her feet and offer your salutations
there. Now raise your eyes and seek the arm holding the
sacred Conch Shell. Strive to grasp and assume the
boundless and undisturbed silence which it signifies. As
the mind attains that mode of peace, draw closer to the
conch and begin to merge with its sleek design. As you
listen intently with all inner faculties finely tuned, perceive the crescendo of a distant sound, as if you are draw-
ing nearer and nearer to an ocean. The distant sound now
becomes an intense humming vibration, as if thousands of
bees are swarming all around you. Om is now distinctly
audible. Perceive it as a living liquidless ocean of potential manifestation, transcending time and space, poised
and waiting for the activating touch of the Creator. As
you envision the Bhagavati Durga Devi raising the sacred
conch to Her lips, contemplate the conch shell's significance with these thoughts:

The Mother is ever-victorious, impossible to defeat!
She exists eternally, ever-immersed in bliss, as Her divine
Conch Shell indicates. The conch is auspiciousness itself,
Her own power of pure inspiration and perpetual triumph.
Yet, wonder of wonders, this exhilarating victory abides
amidst the most perfect calm, all springing from the
Shabda Brahman, the pristine primal vibration. Absolute
Reality is all pure, essentially beyond manifestation, yet
appears as the universe and its living things through the

power inherent in It as conscious vibration! From this comes the cosmic principles of nature such as the elements, their inherent properties, and the power to perceive them called mind and senses. It is all vast, all infinite, all true! Such an intricate design as this infers the existence of a benign Creator!

Now perceive the first impulse set across the living surface of timeless Awareness by the Universal Mother, appearing as a giant wave of creative energy more subtle than thought or life-force, than ether or air, than fire or electricity, than any vibratory manifestation. Know it as the inherent power of Brahman called Shakti. Thrill to the sound of creation as it breaks like waves over the expanding boundaries of an extensive universe, formulating before your inner perception. Be conscious and take note of the Mother's own indivisible existence as pure Consciousness, entering into the physical universe by apparently fragmenting into many pieces and animating a multitude of shapes and forms. Dwell on the endless duration of the conch shell's beautiful tone and listen to its diverse overtones, producing an infinite series of alternate vibrations which appear as the music of the spheres, the spoken and written word, and all the arts and sciences knowable to intelligent beings. Appreciate how She forms, molds, preserves, communicates and transmits this knowledge in and through Her precious human vehicles. Witness, as well, the tone's deterioration as the Mother takes the conch from Her lips, and notice the disappearance of waves and vibrations as all returns to absolute silence. Be aware that ages have passed by in a blink of an eye! An entire cosmic cycle has burst forth from apparent nothingness, sported as living vibration, and dissolved back into its own unseen cause. Mentally and reverently salute the Mother and Her auspicious conch shell and return to normal consciousness with a new understanding of everything around and within you.

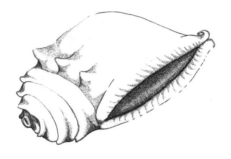

The Discus

Perfection, Totality, Satisfaction, Immediacy, Omniscience.

Meditate on perfection in the form of the Divine Mother's *chakra,* or Discus. Imagine a thing so symmetrical, so complete, so all-containing that nothing is lacking in it. Meditate on its circular design that seems to pulsate and shine with a life all its own. Understand that it represents both form and formlessness, yet intimates what is beyond both, for its shape is contained inside and out by space. Its subtlety makes it a thing of wonder and grace. Now perceive the Bhagavati Durga Devi as She raises the chakra in Her lovely hand. It remains suspended of its own accord, encircling Her shapely finger. It radiates the clear and compassionate light of understanding which is beyond the extent of the average mind to know. As the Mother prepares to unleash it in flight, begin to contemplate the significance of the discus with these thoughts:

The Discus represents perfection, the nature of which is inconceivable to the mind caught in the illusion of relativity. Only within the innermost recesses of the human heart does the intense desire for perfection dwell. By beholding the Universal Mother's Discus, consciousness is transported into a higher state. The mind then yearns for the clarity and vision necessary to awaken the desire for the realization of inherent perfection. The vision of the discus satisfies all other desires and leaves the mind pure and free. It accomplishes its work so fast as to be indiscernible. It appears and disappears so swiftly that consciousness is unaware of its workings, yet the discus itself is aware of all actions throughout the universe and all thoughts within the human mind. It is therefore able to act as the Mother's power of pervasive Omniscience.

Now visualize the Divine Mother's sacred discus as it takes flight and returns to encircle Her blessed finger. Its entire motion is immediate, instantaneous! Understand Consciousness to be like this, all-pervasive and eternal. Now perceive the discus as being one with Her — an extension of Her own being. Thus is it possible for Her to be intrinsically informed about all that it contains. By its existence, design, function and origin, infer that the nature of perfection is immutable, infinite, and eternal — that it can never be changed, diminished or destroyed. Know your own nature to be identical with these qualities and comprehend that this is the ultimate lesson which the *chakra* teaches. The march of events, the appearance of obstacles, the illusion of growth, and the immanence of death — all these are secondary, therefore ultimately unreal. End your meditation with the affirmation that the true Self is all in all, that none else exists. The Mother, Her discus, and Her devoted child are all perfect and self-contained, needing nothing whatsoever from the external realm, for perfection resides within.

The Mala
Spiritual Growth, Supreme Wisdom, Discipline, Concentration, Remembrance, Purification, Transformation, Transcendence, Devotion, Love.

Contemplate the Divine Mother of the Universe gently holding the holy japa mala in Her lovely hand. It is draped across Her beneficent fingers to facilitate the sacred act of mantra recitation. Every bead that She turns spins a world and Her constancy in this sacred art maintains the motion of the planets and animates all living beings. As you visualize this precious scene, be cognizant of the fact that the mala represents the subtle essence of all knowledge. It also signifies the transmission of wisdom through the many revered spiritual teachers gracing all the worlds. Reflect on the far-reaching ramifications of this truth while you offer obeisances to your own spiritual teacher. Now contemplate the significance of the mala with these thoughts:

The mala and recitation of the mantra granted by the precious human teacher bestows the boons of discipline and concentration upon the restless and wayward mind. This in turn makes the path of spiritual growth fruitful and facilitates the attainment of the quality of remembrance, advised by the saints and sages of all religious traditions. Through self-effort, concentration, and remembrance, the process of purification matures and the transformation of human nature takes place, allowing for glimpses of transcendent awareness. When these visions become a more constant occurrence, true devotion, praised most highly by all illumined beings, visits the heart. The mala therefore makes possible the attainment of the highest love which sweeps away all other considerations in a blaze of realization and identity.

At this point, be aware that the mala in your own hand is an extension of the mala gracing Sri Durga's perfect hand. Realize that the motion and constancy of Her concentrated japa is simultaneous with your own. As your visualization becomes stronger, gradually dissolve your individual consciousness into Her supreme state of indivisible awareness. Abide in that condition where no distinctions arise, immersing yourself completely in the essence of the Universal Mother's timeless awareness. As you return to a more relative state of consciousness, retain the awareness that all forms of knowledge, from lower to higher, are manifestations of Her infinite, cosmic mind. Salute the Bhagavati Durga Devi and Her Divine Mala and make the resolve to continually recite the mantra and the holy names for the good of all beings throughout Her creation.

The Bell

*Clarity, Insight, Pure Sound, Attraction and Repulsion,
Realization, and Truth.*

The sacred bell hangs from one of the Divine
Mother's many hands. With the power of your inner
vision, call up this blessed image and concentrate fully
upon it. Begin to analyze its existence and purpose.
Imagine yourself in a huge ancient temple, standing next
to a massive bell. Suddenly it tolls, sending palpable
vibrations through the air for miles. Its intensity produces an immediate change in your body and mind — an
unforgettable sensation! Similar to this intensity, only on
a subtle internal level, the Divine Bell of Sri Durga possesses an innate power that transforms the nature of those
who experience it. Visualize the Universal Mother cast-
ing Her benign glance in your direction, accompanied by
an immense and overpowering wave of subtle bliss. She
intends to sound the bell within your own individual consciousness, removing the many age-old impressions and
inconsistencies that inhabit your mind. As She raises it
for the strike, contemplate the significance of the sacred
bell with these thoughts:

*The sound of the sacred bell brings about absolute and
immediate clarity of mind leading to realization. It is the
death-knell for all negativities that inhabit the conscious
and subconscious levels of the mind. The sound expands
an aspirant's capacity for spiritual insight. To the devotee,
it is the most wonderful and attracting sound, while to the
negative forces that represent the limitations of egotism
and ignorance, the same sound is repulsive and destruc-*

tive. The bell is the Mother's Grace descending in a swift and irreversible fashion, bringing the long sought-after boon of God-realization. It is Truth itself, manifesting through pure sound by the will of the supreme Mother of the Universe.

With your inner ear, perceive the all-pervasive and wonderful sound that emanates from Mother's sacred instrument as it washes over your entire being. Within its vast series of vibrations exists an infinite universe of glorious insights, all transmitted by the captivating and intoxicating voice of the Devi. As these insights enter your consciousness, realize that enlightenment exists at all times. Contemplate this condition of Consciousness and realize it to be easy of access for those who sincerely long for it. Allow this thought to bring you inexpressible joy and become immersed in the realization that you can live moment by moment in the Mother's own divine realm, enjoying Her loving presence perpetually. The thought then occurs that this is the supremely natural condition of awareness for all living beings, either forgotten, sacrificed, or bartered away for a world of impermanent considerations. As the vibrations resolve into deep silence, find yourself sitting once again before your altar, gazing intently at the image of the Universal Mother. The bell rests in its assigned place before you. Intone it purposefully three times for the benefit of all living beings as you remember its profound lessons, chanting *Shantih, Shantih, Shantih.*

The Winecup

Divinity, Immersion and Absorption, Sustenance,
Life-force, Consciousness, Fulfillment, Aspiration,
Immortality.

Focus a clear and eager mind upon the vessel of timeless Immortality which Sri Durga Devi holds in one of Her graceful hands. Divinity itself lies within the cup's recesses. If such an elixir existed on earth, it would be worth more than all the combined wealth of the three worlds! With this thought foremost in mind, and measuring how precious is this nectar, meditate upon the one who drinks daily from this primordial container! Realize that the gods live for ages on just a small drop of this rare liquid. On the other hand, mortals have turned their attention away from it to become enamored with the thin, sour brew of limited existence! Think deeply about the sacred privilege bestowed upon those rare few who leave the mundane realm in search for Immortality, hearing about this marvelous Reality from their precious teachers. With your mind then fixed firmly upon the Mother and Her sacred chalice, contemplate the further significance of the Her Sacred Winecup with these thoughts:

The sacred winecup contains the essence of eternal life. Drinking from it bestows eternal contact and union with the Supreme Being! The individual soul gets merged into the Supreme Soul and experiences the bliss of carefree existence in a condition too ecstatic for description! Life-force and Consciousness — the Mother contains them both — but one is transitory and the other is eternal. Yet, both are Her play through which She grants the fulfillment of all aspirations. Nothing exists outside of Her abundant Reality. The winecup transmits this message and reveals the Universal Mother to be the essence of eternal existence and the sum total of all souls!

The flow of the Mother's Grace is a huge flood, freshly released and rushing in your direction! Imagine yourself to be a huge container able to receive an abundant share of that liquid Grace. It washes over you and inundates your consciousness, saturating it with the elixir of Divine Immortality. What to speak of a drop, an entire cup is now yours to enjoy! Suddenly you realize that you yourself have become the winecup, completely filled, and are resting in the Mother's capable hands. She brings you to Her enchanting lips and empties the drought down Her beautiful throat, leaving you empty like the void! Remain for some time in that condition, absorbed in meditation on formless Reality. Then, once again, you are suddenly deluged and engulfed in an blissful confluence of pure ecstasy. The Mother is filling you again and will eventually empty you according to Her Sweet Will. The realization now dawns upon you that She is the one and only agent of all action, the single yet immeasurable existence, the birth, life, and death of all souls! Gone is your tiny will, and with it passes all limitation forever. Self-surrender is no more a choice. It is now a myth, for there exists only one Divine Self. This one vast existence, a boundless ocean of nectar, is constantly flooding and absorbing in turns, sending streams of souls flowing endlessly across the expanse of an infinite universe. In this perpetual sport, you are but a drop, immersed forever in your immortal nature.

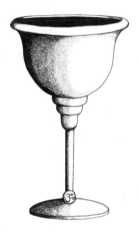

The Shield

Protection, Foresight, Compassion, Concern, Sacrifice,
Perseverance, Refuge, Transmutation, Love.

It is time to learn about true Love. It is laced through and through with the qualities of sacrifice, compassion and constancy. It is devoid of the slightest trace of selfishness or personal motive. It transcends the physical world. Take the Mother's Shield of Complete Protection as your present image for meditation. Envision Her standing behind it, arrayed in gorgeous red silken cloth and swathed in gold. Her shield is impeccable and emanates an aura of invincibility. Contemplating its nature and function, you realize that its outer vibration is one of strength and tenacity, but that this hides its true nature and inner qualities. Penetrating deeper into its significance, the insight dawns that a shield is designed to protect that which is most precious. What could the Divine Mother possibly covet? In the case of the Devi, She holds Her spiritual children most dearly. Her concern is based upon pure Love, a quality seldom experienced or expressed in the physical world. While meditating thus, the qualities contained within the selfless expanse of pure Love become revealed. As the mind becomes immersed in these attributes, contemplate the deeper significance of the shield with these thoughts:

With Her indestructible shield, the Wisdom Mother
protects the entire universe from impending disaster! The
evil intentions of negative forces as well as the ignorant
doings of human beings appear as deep red gashes across
Her fragrant dark skin. On the battlefield of relativity, She

reels but does not fall, and Her ferocity never diminishes! Her sacrifice is stupendous and Her constancy inspirational as She rages incessantly against evil. Such concern for all living beings is beyond understanding. Her shield represents protection, it is true, but the boon of refuge in Her depends upon perseverance. Therefore, She will not stop until all beings are resting in Her, including the demons that oppose Her will. They too will receive refuge, after their misguided and distorted energies get transmuted in the blazing flames of Her purifying fire of all-consuming Love. What a vision is beheld in Her! She epitomizes the true meaning of Love!

As the nature of selfless and long-suffering Love is revealed, continue to meditate upon it with a one-pointed mind. Unite the Mother, Her Love, and Her inspiring sacrifice into one compelling meditation designed to break through the barriers of time, space, and causation and release you from the constraints of limitation forever. Her shield is there to protect you in all endeavors, sacred and secular. Refuge is guaranteed for those who accept the Mother of the Universe as their spiritual ideal. The battle is already won! Eternal victory abides with the Goddess of Divine Love, eternally! As you withdraw from your meditation chant, *Jai Sri Durga Devi ki Jai,* and bow before Her in heartfelt devotion.

The Bow

Projection, Concentration, Strength, Foresight, Will, Discipline.

Meditate upon the auspicious bow of Sri Durga, famed far and wide for its beneficial power. As you envision the beautifully ornate Bow of Perfect Projection held aloft by the Mother of the Universe, contemplate its many fine qualities. Its very presence brings the essential attribute of concentration to bear. Imagine the depth of the Mother's own power of concentration as She enters a state of one-pointed introspection on Divine Reality. Taking an exercise from the Upanishads, envision yourself selecting an arrow of spiritually guided intention from the scabbard of perfect insight. Fit this special arrow into the bow of flawless concentration with the hand of perpetual discipline. Focusing on your target, the nondual Brahman, draw back the arrow carefully with your powerful will. As you concentrate intently on your objective, contemplate the significance of the bow with these thoughts:

The Divine Mother's bow is Her power of one-pointed concentration and perfect projection. Its potential to propel beings towards the highest goal is limitless. Her accuracy in all matters is flawless. Long before the Mother launches Her divine arrows, She is fully confident of the outcome, for Her foresight is based on Omniscience. The bow follows Her every command and projects the dictates of Her sweet will without fail and at Her bidding. It is massive, able to launch many arrows simultaneously, though the strength it takes to draw it is beyond the mind's imagining. It sings Her divine names whenever it is fired and has ancient symbols carved into its polished surface. It launches missiles of love, wisdom, devotion and other fine qualities into the hearts and minds of deserving beings and also sends powerful agents of destruction towards the strongholds of negativity. Beings are awe-struck by its presence and appearance!

Your own consciousness has now become an arrow. The sweet Mother has taken up Her shining bow and is placing you in position. Your will is now Her will, your focus, Her focus. Now your arrow of awareness is being projected towards an objective beyond matter, beyond body, mind and senses, outside the limits of time, space and causality, transcending the universe of name and form. Allow these coverings to fall away, one at a time, as a feeling of greater and greater freedom begins to possess you. You are entering into the boundless expanse of your own true nature, returning to your point of origin, yet you realize you have never been separate from that Source, for it is eternal and all-pervasive. Feel yourself plunging into the very heart of pure Awareness, becoming buried in Its blissful, peaceful expanse. Meditate there for a time.

Reverently salute the bow, the instrument of Mother's Grace that projects and unites consciousness.

The Arrow

Accuracy, Omnipresence, Penetration, Pervasiveness, Impetus, Meticulousness, Unity.

In one of Sri Durga's many lovely hands She holds an auspicious arrow. Settle your mind upon Her wondrous form and seek out that radiant missile. Concentrate upon it as a projectile that never misses its mark, and mentally choose it to be the ideal for every act, thought, word, and deed in your life from this moment forth. Reflect upon the Warrior Goddess and remember how She uses the arrow of penetration in battle, sometimes sending forth hundreds at a time. Realize this phenomena to be both an affirmation of Her presence in all things and an illustration of Her all-knowing, all-seeing nature. Impress upon your mind's awareness that, like the arrows, the Universal Mother is everywhere, permeating everything. Though She holds a single arrow, She is in possession of an infinite supply. This reveals that the many all proceed from the One. Observe that the arrows have all become buried in their respective targets. Understand that this indicates the unity of all things. As insights such as these grace your conscious meditation, contemplate the further significance of the arrow with these thoughts:

The Universal Mother's sacred arrow represents the power of pervasiveness. The arrow is Her penetrating force of intelligence that is at once accurate and meticulous. Whenever thoughts and actions manifest, whenever they bear fruit, wherever they occur, all proceed according to the foresight and insight of the Supreme Goddess. In the uni-

verse, Her arrows are pure shakti power, the many combined powers that create, preserve, and destroy the universe. In the human mind, the arrows represent thoughts, ideas, intentions and other impulses. As spiritual aids, they are aspirations, intuitions, insights and direct perception. In short, the Divine Mother's arrows are everywhere, all pointing towards immersion and unity. Her deluge of arrows representing divine qualities inundate human consciousness, transforming it in an instant! Individualized awareness is one of Her penetrating arrows, utilized for the benefit of all beings. She drives many such arrows deep into the heart of the Ultimate Being, absorbing them forever into one eternal and divine essence.

At this juncture in your meditation, feel the Divine Mother's attention upon you at all levels of your being, as if a shower of arrows has penetrated every aspect of your life. As a result you are overcome with a familiar yet astonishing sense of the interconnectedness of all things. Even the distinction between inner and outer modes of awareness has seemed to dissolve, leaving one cohesive existence everywhere. With your eyes open or closed, whether moving or stationary, whether awake or asleep, the experience of an unfragmented and eternal consciousness remains constant, filling you with subtle bliss. As periods of activity arise in due course, all seems to proceed with ease and efficiency, making you aware of the existence of the Mother's Grace, Her benign hand guiding you through all actions and duties. Marvel at this ineffable condition and compare it to the usual way you live and think. Resolve to retain this exalted experience to the best of your ability, realizing that it is the Universal

Mother's normal and continual state of mind. Reverently salute Her as the essence of conscious Awareness abiding in all things and humbly prostrate to all Her manifestations.

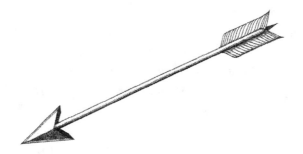

The Spear

Penetration, Omnipotence, Courage, Light, Wisdom, Creativity.

At the forefront of your mental image of Sri Durga is the spear, which dominates the scene. This respected weapon now captivates your attention and draws you into one-pointed concentration upon its qualities. Admiring its grand design, you notice the ornate carvings and inlays which gracefully cover its surface. You realize what a great boon it is just to lay eyes upon it. An ancient and primeval aura emanates from it which gives it the mystique of timelessness and power. It is a weapon that has been driven deep into the thickest realms of ignorance, dealing a death blow to the ego of countless negative beings. The realization then dawns that the Mother uses it for battles involving the direst of circumstances. Together with Her wisdom sword, the spear is Her most aggressive weapon. This brings to mind Her undaunted courage, even in the face of the most ferocious adversity. Contemplate the nature of this courage springing from the spear's image. Embrace this quality within your own heart and feel its unfailing support. As you implement this divine attribute into your being, turn and face your most powerful inner adversary. Ruminate upon the presence of any old or new problem or obstacle that has plagued your existence while simultaneously holding the Mother's spear of penetrating courage. As you maintain this attitude of introspection, contemplate the further significance of the spear with these thoughts:

The Divine Mother is Omnipotent and Her influence and authority are absolute. Her proud spear is indestructible and invincible! There is no force in the universe that can withstand its power for ultimate good. The Divine Mother's devoted children are Her manifestations, and as such represent so many spears of penetrating awareness. What inner obstacle or negativity could possibly thwart them since Her stainless presence abides within. They are ever-one with the spear's purpose. With it they can plumb the depths of the subconscious mind, destroying all negative influences that may be hiding there. As a result they emerge as supreme warriors of Truth, surrounded by light and immersed in glory! Their divine nature is pure and without taint. Nothing can corrode or mar them in any way. The expansive field of awareness is now cleared and fertile for planting. Wherever the spear falls within this hallowed ground, a sublime experience manifests. All is guided by the supreme will of the Universal Mother who has provided everything. Salutations to the Warrior Goddess, the Wisdom Mother, the essence of all gods and goddesses! Salutations, salutations, salutations again and again!

As you emerge from your powerful meditation, retain the light of pure awareness that has begun to shine as a result of your act of courage. Envision this light all around you, inside of you and permeating the entire universe. See it extending beyond into the realms of angelic beings and all the way up to the highest realm of nondual Truth. Each deathless ray of light is a radiant, golden spear, extending throughout the three worlds and fourteen realms of existence. Each spear of light is a distilled and compressed flash of wisdom, capable of blossoming forth as extensive and unique expressions of knowledge. This copious knowledge, which burgeons as creative genius, gets disseminated to the worlds as various systems of learning. Meditate on this expressive creativity as the only true intoxicant for the intellect. Its presence in the form of spiritual insight is now adding an entirely new dimension to your mind in spontaneous fashion. This informs you that Truth is eternal, pervasive, and ever-present, not something that is discovered or created. Absorb your mind in this profound thought and realize its vast implications. Your mind, in a purified state, is the infinite repository of all wisdom, possessing the ability and capacity for sacred creative expression. As you finish your meditation on the Mother's spear, resolve to access the untapped potential of your mind based upon devotion to the Warrior Goddess and service to all living beings. Salute the Wisdom Mother with all sincerity — She who is the eternal fountain of creative energy and the essence of absolute Truth.

Notes

1   Excerpt from Lex Hixon's translation of Ramprasad's song, "Mono Boli Bhaja Kali," from the album *Kali Bol* by Jai Ma Music.

2   Quotations from Ramprasad Sen are from a manuscript of expanded translations of the poet/saint by Lex Hixon.

3   *Srimad Devi Bhagavatam*, Swami Vijnanananda trans., Munshiram Manoharlal Publishers Pvt. Ltd.

4   Illusory superimposition, also called "false superimposition," is a misreading of Reality due to the mind's ignorance. Absolute Reality is pure, infinite and eternal — never limited by the material universe or the thoughts of living beings. Therefore, to the discriminating aspirant, all forms and concepts are seen as coverings over Reality which seem to obscure or modify Its essence, like different colored sheets of glass which apparently transform one clear light into various hues. As one light appears as many colors, so too does one Consciousness reflect through countless beings, yet their minds and senses, as limiting adjuncts, express only a modicum of its boundless nature.

5   The six passions are lust, anger, greed, delusion, pride and envy.

6   *"The Nine Limbs of Devotion According to Sri Ram,"* by Babaji Bob Kindler.

7   The idea here is that the bija, Hrim, is an extremely subtle representation of the Absolute. It is the Divine Mother's channel or conduit, as it were,

through which Her many sublime energies flow and
get transmitted to others. Originating from an
unmanifest state, She causes and permeates existence, appearing as the force of will, the power of
intelligence and the inclination to act (Shakti power
which is all-pervasive in Absolute, Transcendent
and Imminent modes — Its immutable essence, Its
ability to perceive/conceive and Its love of expressive sport). At the manifest level of the sequential
line, the same power appears as prana which forms
the five elements and their inherent properties,
again from subtlest to the least subtle.

8   Ramprasad Poem #307 from the Jai Ma Music
album, *The Ecstatic Songs of Ramprasad,* translated
by Lex Hixon.

9   *Ishavasyopanishad.*

Glossary

Advaita — Nondual philosophy of absolute unity without compromise, brought into prominence by the great philosopher Adishankaracharya.

Advaitan — One who lives by and prescribes to the Advaita philosophy.

Advaitic — Non-dual in content; of the nature of nonduality and having to do with Advaita Philosophy.

Agni — The god of fire in Vedic times; fire.

Aim — A sacred bija or seed mantra infused with the power of wisdom and its transmission.

Akasha — Subtle space; one of the five elements of Prakriti out of which the universe is fashioned.

Anahata dhvani — Om, or the "Sound Brahman." The "unstruck sound" heard by the yogis at the time of spiritual awakening and meditation.

Apana — Prana which governs the intestinal region and aids in the evacuation of waste from the body.

Asuras — Powerful beings who vie for supremacy with the gods; negative forces or demons.

Atman — The eternal Soul residing within every being, which is birthless, deathless, pure, and perfect by nature.

Avatar — One who descends; the appearance of Divinity in human form; an incarnation of God.

Avyakrita — The unmodified, undifferentiated, undefined — a condition of Absolute Reality.

Avyakta — The unmanifested—a condition of Absolute Reality; state of complete equilibrium.

Bhagavati — The Supreme Being manifest as the Mother of the Universe.

Bhakti — Devotion for the Supreme Lord.

Bija — A seed syllable which forms an essential part of a mantra and which invokes the presence of God through a particular mode or aspect.

Bija mantra — The mantra accompanied by its empowering elements.

Bindu — The Mahat-tattva; the initial seed from whence all things are born; concentrated point; dot; source.

Bindu, nada, kalatita — The initial seed, the primal sound and the web of time, implying what is beyond all three.

Brahma — The first aspect of the Hindu Trinity who represents the power of creation.

Brahma, Vishnu, Shiva — Emanations of Ishvara; anthropomorphic gods representing and in charge of the cosmic functions of creation, preservation and destruction.

Brahmajnana — The highest knowledge of Paravidya; realization of Brahman.

Brahman — The Absolute; the Ultimate Reality; formless Essence.

Buddhi — Intelligence; one of the four parts of Antahkarana, the mental sheath or human mind according to Samkhya and Vedanta.

Chaitanya — Pure and Absolute Consciousness without modifications that knows all things.

Chakra — Spiritual vortex or center, of which there are seven according to the science of Kundalini Yoga, located in the subtle body associated with the spinal column; a divine weapon particularly associated with Vishnu and His primordial Shakti.

Chandi — *The Devi Mahatmyam.* A holy scripture of over 700 mantrams describing and pertaining to the Divine Mother of the Universe.

Daya — Compassion, especially associated with the removal of suffering and specifically the ignorance which causes it.

Devas — The gods who reflect the powers of the Supreme Being.

Devi Mahatmyam — One of the authoritative sacred texts of Divine Mother worship.

Devis — The goddesses who reflect the powers of the Supreme Being.

Durga — The Divine Mother of the Universe; the ten-armed Goddess who is the essence of all gods and goddesses; the first of five main aspects of the Universal Mother (Prakriti Panchaka) according to the *Srimad Devi Bhagavatam.*

Durgama — A name for the Divine Mother Durga which She received due to defeating a demon of that name.

Durgasaptasati — The many collected mantras pertaining to Sri Durga; also called the *Devi Mahatmyam* and the *Chandi.*

Gaudapada - The quintessential Advaita philosopher, said to be the guru of the guru of Adishankaracharya.

Guru — Revered spiritual preceptor.

Hrillekha — A formal name for the bija syllable, Hrim.

Hrim or Hring — A powerful bija or seed syllable representing the power of purification, transformation, beauty, and Grace.

Iccha shakti — That aspect of Divine Mother power

which comprises Her indomitable will. It is omnipotence personified.

Indra — The Lord of the gods; the foremost among the lesser powers of the Supreme Being.

Ishta — The chosen ideal; that which the devotee accepts as the highest standard in spiritual life.

Ishvara — The supreme and most comprehensive aspect of Divinity residing within the universe who oversees its various lesser powers and their functions.

Ishvari — The supreme power of the universe in a feminine aspect.

Itihasa — Spiritual history and mythology of India, especially reflected in the *Mahabharata, Ramayana,* and other famous texts.

Jai — Victory; the triumph of the spiritual over the mundane.

Japa — The efficacious practice of silently reciting the sacred mantra or names of God while turning the holy beads (mala).

Japa mala — The rosary or sacred beads.

Jnana — Knowledge; spiritual wisdom associated with the path of discrimination which benefits spiritual life.

Jnana shakti — That aspect of Divine Mother power which comprises Her all-seeing, all-knowing Wisdom. It is omniscience personified.

Kaitabha — A particularly ferocious demon (asura) destroyed by Mother Durga.

Kalatita — The concept of time and what lies beyond it as its witness.

Kali — A supreme name for the Divine Mother of the Universe as the Deva/Devi Swarupaya—the essence of all gods and goddesses; She who personifies time and acts as a witness to the phenomenal march of events contained in it; The Divine Mother of the Universe in Her four-armed form, worshipped by Sri Ramakrishna Paramahamsa; Lord Shiva's dynamic power and eternal consort.

Karandamukuta — The hairpiece crown worn by gods and goddesses.

Karma — Good and bad action and its results; residual effects appearing in the life of embodied beings due to past and present activities.

Karma yogini/yogi — One who is perfect in works and ever-free from their effects.

Kriya — Spontaneous action; physical action such as exercises in Hatha Yoga.

Kriya Shakti — That aspect of Mother power which comprises Her dynamic, spontaneous and ever-expressive nature. It is omnipresence personified.

Kundalini — The powerful yet subtle spiritual force that when awakened brings illumination to all levels of being.

Loka — Realm, or world.

Madhu — A particularly ferocious demon (asura) destroyed by Lord Vishnu.

Mahabharata — A great Hindu epic containing hundreds of stories dealing with earthly and religious life and their interconnections.

Mahalila — The great play or sport of Consciousness; the cosmic theater with all beings as actors and actresses.

Mahamaya — The grand illusion; the superimposition of the universe and its constituents over Brahman;

the One who conjures up the grand illusion.

Mahashakti — The great Shakti in Her role of creator, preserver, and destroyer of the universe of name and form.

Maheshvara — The Supreme Lord of the Worlds.

Manus — The first-born children of Brahma, the God of creation.

Medha — Retentive memory; subtle intelligence, especially associated with matters of a spiritual nature.

Mula Prakriti — Literally, root nature. The foundation of the Created universe implying its Creator, in this case, the Divine Mother of the Universe, the source and origin of all manifestation.

Muni — A sage possessing clear insight on spiritual matters; a sage observing silence (mauna).

Mala — A string of sacred beads, like a rosary, used primarily for mental repetition of the Holy Names of God.

Mantra — A powerful formula consisting of seed syllables and Holy Names which the initiate uses to purify the mind and invoke the presence of God within the self.

Maya — Illusion; the projecting and veiling power of Brahman which causes the appearance and disappearance of the universe.

Maya shabala — The subtle power of Shakti that is somehow able to divide something of unified origin into many apparent parts.

Mayavadin — One who ascribes to the philosophy that declares the entire universe of name and form to be illusory or unreal. Also known as Mithyavada.

Nine Limbs of Bhakti — The nine statements of Sri

Ramachandra utilized for the attainment of devotion to God.

Om or Aum — The quintessential bija mantra epitomizing transcendent perfection; the unstruck sound or primal vibration from which the creation springs.

Padma — Literally the lotus; an especially revered name for Sri Lakshmi, the Goddess of abundance.

Pippilada — An ancient Rishi mentioned in the Vedic scriptures.

Prakriti — Nature; causal matter; the universe of name and form and those ingredients which comprise it; the pradhana of Samkhya which corresponds to the Maya of Vedanta with these main distinctions — it exists independent of Spirit and it is considered real.

Prakriti Panchaka — An appellation referring to the Divine Mother of the Universe as the five main powers of Shakti who together constitute Divine Reality in its dynamic mode. The five aspects are Durga, Lakshmi, Saraswati, Savitri, and Radha.

Pralaya — Dissolution of the phenomenal universe after an extremely long cycle of time.

Prana — Subtle energy; life-force; vital being; the subtle force from which all mental and physical energy has evolved.

Pranas — The five "subtle winds" or functions of prana called prana, apana, vyana, udana, and samana.

Prasnopanisad — One of the sacred scriptures of Vedanta which forms a part of the knowledge portion (Brahmakanda) of the Vedas, concerned solely with the realization of the Soul (Atman).

Prema — Ecstatic love for God that causes forgetfulness

of everything transitory.

Puranas — Ancient scriptures illustrating the lives of Avatars, saints, and sages; 18 in number: six to Brahma, six to Vishnu, and six to Shiva.

Ramayana — A Hindu epic like the *Mahabharata,* containing many stories and teachings of a practical and spiritual nature, whose hero is Sri Ram.

Ramprasad — A Bengali poet/saint of the 14th century who was a devotee of Mother Kali and whose songs inspired many beings including Sri Ramakrishna Paramahamsa, who used them to illustrate spiritual truths.

Rishis — Illumined beings from ancient times who practiced extreme austerities in order to receive the truths contained in the Vedas and Upanishads. Most were married and of both sexes and passed their wisdom orally to their children.

Sadhana — Spiritual disciplines undertaken to realize God.

Samadhi — Supersensual spiritual experience.

Samana — One of the five pranas whose specific function is to control the digestive process.

Samskaras — Positive and negative latent impressions in the subconscious and unconscious mind that shape human character, caused by repetitious actions through many lifetimes.

Sanatana Dharma — The Eternal Religion of the ancients; eternal Truth which is never conceived of or forgotten but is ever-existent.

Sanskrit — An ancient language, Vedic or pre-Vedic in origin, often called the language of the gods.

Saraswati — The Goddess of art and learning; one of

the five main aspects of the Universal Mother (Prakriti Panchaka).

Satchitananda — Pure Being, pure Consciousness, pure Bliss absolute; a name for the formless Brahman.

Satchitananda Vigraha — The Absolute as the origin of all Beings, sentient or insentient.

Sattva Shuddha — Beyond even the highest guna (sattva); exceedingly pure; of the very nature of purity.

Savitri — One of the five main aspects of Divine Mother Reality whose special attributes comprise, among others, various branches of wisdom (vedangas), mantras and the Holy Names.

Shabda Brahman — The sound Brahman; God as subtle vibration.

Shakti — The creative force of the universe which is the active principle of Brahman yet identical with It.

Shastras — The scriptures.

Shiva — The third deity in the Hindu Trinity; the God of Wisdom who dissolves the universe of name and form at the end of cosmic cycles.

Simhavahini — She who rides the lion; a name for Bhagavati Durga Devi.

Smriti — Memory; code of law; auxiliary scriptures supporting the Vedas and Upanishads (shruti).

Sri Ramakrishna — The Kali Avatar; the God-realized master of 19th century India, generally accepted as the Divine Incarnation of this age.

Sristhi — Projection; associated with the creative power of God called Shakti.

Sthiti — Preservation or sustenance; associated with the creative power of God called Shakti.

Sura — A divine being; a god.

Surya — The sun; the god of the sun.

Tattva — Cosmic principles; in Samkhya philosophy, a term for twenty-four constituents of Prakriti which make up the universe of name and form.

Udana — One of the five pranas functioning in the human body that controls the functions of the upper body and aids in the coalescence of the physical, mental and spiritual aspects of life.

Upanishads — The Brahmakanda portion of the Vedas dealing with the knowledge that confirms Truth and reveals the Atman.

Vedas — The four ancient scriptures of Sanatana Dharma which are eternal, without beginning, and not ascribed to human authorship.

Vidya — Knowledge, usually pertaining to matters of a spiritual nature.

Vishnu — The second deity in the Hindu Trinity; the God of preservation and the one from whom the Avatars emerge.

Vishnu Maya — The enchanting power of the Supreme Being which causes illusory manifestations such as matter, name, and form to appear lasting and absolute; the *Mayashakti* of Lord Vishnu which is His very essence.

Vija — See *bija*.

Vyana — The energy of *prana* that deals with the circulation of the blood.

Sources and Books for Further Reading

Srimad Devi Bhagavatam, translated by Swami Vijnanananda. This amazing book of over 1000 pages is one of the few quintessential scriptures on the Divine Mother. We are sincerely grateful for Swami Vijnanananda's tremendous effort and contribution by translating this important text, and to the publishers for making it available for the Western devotees of the Divine Mother. Published by Munshiram Manoharlal Publishers Pvt. Ltd. P.O. Box 5715, 54 Rani Jhansi Road, New Delhi 110 055

Devi Mahatmyam, also known as the *Chandi*, a collection of 700 mantras in praise of the Divine Mother of the Universe. This scripture is available in many translations and concerns Mother Durga's victorious campaigns against the negative forces *(Asuras)*.

Divine Mother of the Universe, Visions of the Goddess and Tantric Hymns of Enlightenment, by Lex Hixon, Quest Books. Expanded translations of songs to the Divine Mother, by Ramprasad Sen, a 14th century poet/saint.

The Ecstatic Songs of Ramprasad, vol. I. The inspiring poetry of Ramprasad, translated by Lex Hixon, is set to music on this album by Jai Ma Music, P.O.Box 380, Paauilo, HI 96776

Sri Sarada Vijnanagita, by Babaji Bob Kindler, the wisdom words of Sri Sarada Devi rendered in poetic verse.

Those interested in the Wisdom Teachings of the Divine Mother Path and Sanatana Dharma (Eternal Truth) are invited to write or phone:

SRV Oregon
P.O. Box 14012
Portland, OR 97293
(503) 774-2410
srvinfo@srv.org

SRV San Francisco
465 Brussels Street
San Francisco, CA 94134
(415) 468-4680
hcsrv@yahoo.com

SRV Hawaii Retreat Center
P.O. Box 380
Paauilo, HI 96776
srvhawaiirc@srv.org

or visit our website at www.SRV.org